# He Kept the Colors

## The true story of

## The General,
## the Old Man and the Flag

A Factual Account of
Color Sergeant Thomas Henry Sheppard,
Co. E. 1st Michigan Cavalry,
Union Forces of the Civil War

**Written by L. E. Johnson**

Bloomington, IN          authorHOUSE®          Milton Keynes, UK

*AuthorHouse™*
*1663 Liberty Drive, Suite 200*
*Bloomington, IN 47403*
*www.authorhouse.com*
*Phone: 1-800-839-8640*

*AuthorHouse™ UK Ltd.*
*500 Avebury Boulevard*
*Central Milton Keynes, MK9 2BE*
*www.authorhouse.co.uk*
*Phone: 08001974150*

*First published by AuthorHouse 6/14/2007*

*ISBN: 978-1-4259-9088-6 (sc)*
*ISBN: 978-1-4259-9087-9 (hc)*

*Printed in the United States of America*
*Bloomington, Indiana*

*This book is printed on acid-free paper.*

*Library of Congress Control Number: 2007900340*

* In order for this book to be written, <u>every part of it</u> had to come from other people's accounts. I am grateful to the pages of the Marlette Leader, to the Marlette District Library, and to the Sons of Union Veterans of the Civil War, John S. Cosbey Camp #427 in Dearborn, Michigan, and especially to Commander Jerry Olson and Rick Danes for sharing the narrative given to them by Thomas Henry Sheppard's grandson, Lawrence, and for allowing me to use their materials as needed, as well as the information on the Detroit Arsenal. Thanks also to Daryl Wilson for sharing the Sheppard Family papers. I am grateful to my friends Jean Morgan and Delphine Vizard for proofreading; to Glenn and Carol Jamison for technical help; and to Ron Barrons for the beautiful cover design...also to my mother's best friend from high school, Leola Sheppard M<sup>c</sup>Vean, and to her daughter, Linda Moore, my friend, who first told me that my "old man and the flag" was their great-grandfather. Thomas was a very colorful character. I found many discrepancies and am reminded of this:

## "The past really happened. History is just what somebody wrote down."
*(unknown)*


## "How fickle the threads of historical accuracy."
-Judge Lincoln and James Donahue, <u>Fiery Trial.</u>


## It is from our past we create our future.


## <u>"The Land of the Free--Because of the Brave."</u>
-Lt. Colonel Fitzpatrick & the 336<sup>th</sup> Combat Air Patrol
Speaking to Rush Limbaugh--June 2006

# Dedication

In memory of President Abraham Lincoln,
Commander-In-Chief of the Union Forces during the Civil War,
and mindful of his request for America--that
"This nation UNDER GOD shall have a new birth of freedom"...

In memory of General Ulysses S. Grant,
the greatest General, my relative...

*In memory of Color Sgt. Thomas Henry Sheppard,*
*one of the greatest volunteer soldiers of them all...*

*In memory of General John (Black Jack) Logan,*
*the greatest volunteer soldier of all...*

*In memory of Michigan's own
General George Armstrong Custer...*

# Dedication (continued)

<u>To our great Commander-in-Chief, President George W. Bush...</u>

To everyone who ever served in the military service

of the United States of America...

To each and every volunteer soldier...

To every soldier who died in action...

To every soldier Missing In Action...

To every soldier taken Prisoner of War...

**To my own personal POW/MIA bracelet honoree**

**Lt. Col. Bruce Gardner Johnson of Harbor Beach, Michigan,**

**Advisor at Ben Cat Province...**

**the longest unaccounted for POW/MIA regular Army**

in Vietnam War; Date Missing: June 10, 1965--Xoai Battle...

**"I have carried you on eagles' wings and brought you here to me."**

**-Exodus 19:4**

To my brother, U. S. Army SGT. E5 Charles D. Johnson,

Recon. Squad Leader, Vietnam...

To Rush Limbaugh for his unwavering

loyalty and respect for America's soldiers every day...

To Paralyzed Veterans of America...

To Disabled Veterans of America...

To Veterans of Foreign Wars...

To Amvets, where every day is Veterans Day...

To the SONS OF UNION VETERANS OF THE CIVIL WAR,

Department of Michigan

Sgt. John S. Cosbey Camp 427 (SUVCW)-

Commander Jerry Olson & Rick Danes

Dearborn Historical Commission,

Detroit Arsenal;

Commandant's Quarters

(from which Thomas Henry Sheppard and the 1st Michigan Cavalry

received their gear and guns, and where his flag rests now)

The flag made by the women of the Marlette area and carried by Thomas Henry Sheppard had 34 stars. It survived 13 major battles and over one hundred skirmishes. It went through 16 months of war and bore 72 bullet holes. It survived 505 days of prison in several prisons of the South, including, according to an interview with Mr. Sheppard himself in the Detroit Free Press: Libby Prison, Belle Isle, Savannah, Charlotte, Andersonville, Goldsboro, Macon, the government shops in Georgia & Mellans Stockade.

## (Author's Note)

Back in 1985, I came across the story of General Logan, the Old Man, and the Flag in the pages of the old *Marlette Leader* newspapers. Many years later, I began my research into the annals of the Civil War for the rest of Thomas Henry Sheppard's story. I also faced a search for the current whereabouts of the Battle Flag of Company E, First Michigan Cavalry, Union Forces of the Civil War. I was overwhelmed by the vast amounts of information I had myself forgotten about the Civil War.

Assuming that many of you who read this story are not authorities on the Civil War, I am including as part of my story every interesting bit of information that caught my eye and shed light on Thomas' story...songs, poems, facts...always assuming, of course, the authenticity of my sources. There is no doubt that you will see the parallels between then and now. This is not just another account about the Civil War...it is the incredible story of an amazing coincidence involving a very famous general and an old man in the tiny town of Marlette, Michigan, and a flag made by the women of my town. And it turned into so much more. I myself will never again think the same of Gettysburg, for now I will always see in my mind the blissful faces of those happy horses knee-deep in clover, garlands of flowers thrown around their necks by the happy girls of the town, while the Michigan men were being stuffed with fragrant breads covered with apple butter.

Every time a soldier dies,

There are Tears in Heaven...

GOD's Tears

# The Civil War Song
## "We Are Coming Father Abraham"

*If you look across the hill-tops that meet the Northern sky,*
*Long moving lines of rising dust your vision may descry;*
*And now the wind, an instant, tears the cloudy veil aside,*
*And floats aloft our spangled flag in glory and in pride;*
*And bayonets in the sunlight gleam, and bands brave music pour--*
*"We are coming Father Abraham--three hundred thousand more!"*

"Love your country and live with pride
And don't forget those who died–America, can't you see?
All gave some...Some gave all.
Some stood through for the red, white and blue,
And some had to fall.
And if you ever think of me
Think of all your liberties and recall
**Some gave all.**"

--Billy Ray Cyrus
"SOME GAVE ALL"

# The Gettysburg Address

Four score and seven years ago our fathers brought forth
on this continent a new nation, conceived in liberty and
dedicated to the proposition that all men are created equal.
Now we are engaged in a great civil war,
testing whether that nation,
or any nation so conceived and so dedicated, can long endure.
We are met on a great battlefield of that war.
We have come to dedicate a portion of
that field, as a final resting place
for those who here gave their lives that that nation might live.
It is altogether fitting and proper that we should do this.
But in a larger sense, we cannot dedicate--
we cannot consecrate--we cannot hallow--this ground.
The brave men, living and dead, who
struggled here, have consecrated it,
far above our poor power to add or detract.
The world will little note, nor long remember, what we say here,
but it can never forget what they did here.
It is for us, the living, rather to be here
dedicated to the unfinished work
which they who fought here have thus far so nobly advanced.
It is rather for us to be here dedicated to the
great task remaining before us--
that from these honored dead we take increased devotion
to that cause for which they gave the last full measure of devotion--
that we here highly resolve that these dead
shall not have died in vain--
that this nation, under God, shall have a new birth of freedom--
and that government of the people, by the people, for the people,
shall not perish from the earth.

--Abraham Lincoln

# FACTS OF THE CIVIL WAR

*The War Department spent $4 million a year on bands.*
*In July of 1862 there were 618 bands in service*
*or 1 musician to every 41 soldiers.*

☆☆☆

There were 40,000 musicians in the Union army.

☆☆☆

Ulysses S. Grant was only 39 years old in 1861.

☆☆☆

Ulysses S. Grant's mother, Hannah Simpson, and my great-great-grandmother, Fannie Simpson, were sisters.

☆☆☆

In August of 1863, W. C. Quantrill and his Raiders terrorized the West.  The infamous Younger Boys and a youthful Jesse James and older brother Frank rode with Quantrill, although Jesse was too young to enlist at the beginning of the war.

☆☆☆

Johnson's Island was a Union prison for Confederate prisoners, officers in particular, located three miles out in Lake Erie north of the city of Sandusky, Ohio, and ½ mile south of Marblehead Peninsula.  It was a 300 acre island with a view of Canada on one side and Ohio on the other.  It was open 40 months with flimsy temporary buildings which held 10-15,000 prisoners, while made for only 1000.
**\* \* One hundred years later, quarry workers at Johnson's Island are haunted by the song, "Dixie", in the late afternoon when the sun begins to go down...*perhaps the Men in Gray are not all resting in peace here.***

☆☆☆

*More than 3,700 Union soldiers killed at Gettysburg are buried at the Soldiers' National Monument, which commemorates the Union dead.*

✩✩✩

In the Shenandoah Valley Campaign of 1862, the 16,000 men of Stonewall Jackson marched more than 600 miles in 35 days, fighting five major battles, and defeating four separate Union armies totaling 63,000 men.

✩✩✩

George Armstrong Custer, the Boy General, became a Major General in 1865 at the age of 25.  He set a record that has yet to be broken.

✩✩✩

*The Union had 90 gunboats when the war came; the South had none.*

✩✩✩

*Federal observation balloons (new) such as the hydrogen-filled "Intrepid" provided accurate information on Confederate battlefield movements.*

✩✩✩

Horace L. Hunley had a prototype submarine (new) at Charleston in 1863.  It was propelled by eight men operating hand cranks, and could make 4 mph.  On February 17, 1864, it attacked the Union sloop *Housatonic* in Charleston Harbor and sent her to the bottom, making it the first warship in history to be sunk by a submarine.  The crew of the *Hunley* perished in the explosion, making the crew the first crew of a submarine to die in war.

✩✩✩

The ironclad warships (new) would change the course of naval history, although they did not seriously affect the outcome of this war. The two most famous in this war were the *USS Monitor* and the *USS Merrimac.*

✩✩✩

*The railroad (new) played a vital role in this war, for the first time in history.  The rails carried men, horses, material to the front.*

✩✩✩

Lincoln walked daily to the telegraph (new) office in the War Department across from the White House. "I come here to escape my persecutors," he told the operators. There he received news of the armies and wrote out replies to his generals.

☆☆☆

*The Federal Ordnance men turned down the Spencer repeating breech-loading rifle in 1860, as they thought the soldiers would fire too fast and waste ammunition. The troops did not get them until late in the war. The outcome may not have changed, but it might have been over sooner.*

☆☆☆

*Innovations and inventions of the beginning of modern warfare included all of the above new plus: periscopes; exploding shells; trenches; snorkel; land-mines; naval torpedoes; telescopic sights for rifles; Taps; long-range rifles; machine guns; legal voting for servicemen; U.S. Secret Service; Income and Withholding Tax; Tobacco & Cigarette tax; the draft; bread lines; Medal of Honor; Press Correspondences; Battle photos.*

☆☆☆

*Eight Federal generals came from the small town of Galena, Illinois, and owed their rank to Ulysses S. Grant, Galena's most famous citizen, who also was the very first ever General of the Army.*

☆☆☆

*\*\* On the average, each Confederate man shot required 240# powder and 900# lead. \*\**

☆☆☆

The first organized aerial psychological warfare: dropping of Lincoln's Amnesty Proposal behind Southern lines by kites.

☆☆☆

*The gallant 24th Michigan was recruited in Wayne County in Detroit and was part of the Iron Brigade. It was one of the first Union regiments to see action at Gettysburg. On July 1, 1863, it unfortunately was to become known as the Union Regiment with the highest casualty rate of any Union army at Gettysburg, having lost 316 killed and wounded.*

☆☆☆

Confederate General Nathan Bedford Forrest, whom historians call "the war's most able cavalry commander", had 29 horses shot out from under him.  He went on to found the Ku Klux Klan.

✩✩✩

*Many years before the war Jesse Grant, the father of General U. S. Grant, lived and worked in the home of Owen Brown, whose small son grew up to be John Brown, the Abolitionist martyr who lit the fuse to war.*

✩✩✩

Seven former Union generals served as President of the United States:
Chester Arthur
James A. Garfield
Ulysses S. Grant
Benjamin Harrison
Rutherford B. Hayes
Andrew Johnson
William McKinley
One former U. S. Vice-President fought for the
Confederacy at Lynchburg as a general:
John Breckinridge

✩✩✩

The *U.S.S. Michigan* was for many years the only American ship of war on the Great Lakes. Launched at Erie, Pennsylvania in 1844, she patrolled to guard the prison on Johnson's Island.

✩✩✩

*The first plantation mansion seized in the war by the Union belonged to Mrs. Robert E. Lee.*

✩✩✩

*The highest ranking civilian to volunteer for service in the war was Vice President Hannibal Hamlin.*

✩✩✩

*Harper Hospital in Detroit opened on October 12, 1864, as a military hospital.*

✩✩✩

Soldiers traditionally marched into battle while
their bands played martial music.
In the Civil War, the band was at the head of the column,
while the bells of brass instruments were pointed to
the rear so the troops could hear clearly.

✮✮✮

*12,912 Union prisoners died at Andersonville
Prison and were buried nearby.
211,400 Union soldiers were taken prisoner, while
30,208 of them did not survive prison.
Confederate prisoners amounted to 462,000
including those in the final surrender.
25,976 were dead in prison.*

✮✮✮

The bloodiest day in American history was September 17, 1862,
at Antiedam, where  23,000 men fell that day.

✮✮✮

*"Chickamauga" is a Cherokee word meaning "river of death".*

✮✮✮

The military draft was used first in this war, by both sides.

✮✮✮

*Of the 2,300,000 men in the Union army,
70% were under the age of 23...
100,000 were only 16...another 100,000 were 15 years old.
Three hundred were only 13 years old or less,
and 25 were under the age of 10.*

✮✮✮

More than 620,000 soldiers lost their lives in the Civil War--
260,000 Confederate soldiers and 360,000 Union men.

✮✮✮

*More Union and Confederate soldiers died In the Civil War
than in all other United States wars combined, including Vietnam.*

✮✮✮

During May and June of 1864,
Union armies in Virginia lost 77,452 men…
more men that Lee had in his entire army.

☆☆☆

*Lee's men in 1863 got a month's worth of rations: a small
amount of dried fruit; a few peas; 18 ounces of flour;
less than a pound of bacon; ten pounds of rice.*

☆☆☆

In the assault on Petersburg in 1864,
604 of the Federal regimental troops were wounded
or killed in less than 20 minutes.

☆☆☆

The Civil War is known for its medical care:
pus was considered a good sign; nothing was sterilized;
no one really knew why wounds became infected.
Diarrhea and dysentery alone killed 44,558 Union soldiers.
Twice as many men died from disease as from enemy bullets.
Maggots were considered good, as they feasted
on bad tissue and left the good alone.

☆☆☆

*A private was paid $13.00 a month.
A colonel was paid $95.00 a month.
A Brigadier General was paid $124.00 monthly.
A musket cost $13.00.*

☆☆☆

According to the Civil War Sourcebook, when the war started
there were more than 22 million people in the North;
the South had 9 million, with more than a third slaves.

☆☆☆

*Ninety percent of the manufacturing was in the North.
Most of the copper, precious metals, iron and coal
and 2/3rd 's of the railroad miles were also in the North.*

☆☆☆

12 percent of the Union Army, during the last three years of the war, were black.  More than 1/3 of their total enlistment died.  Twenty-one black soldiers were awarded the Medal of Honor.

✰✰✰

*The 16th North Carolina Infantry at Gettysburg went into battle with about 800 men.  Three days later, 92 were left, with the rest dead, missing, or wounded.  This gave them the distinction of "The Greatest Regimental Loss in a Single Battle."*
*In that same regiment, in one company of 84 men,*
*each and every man, officers included, was hit.*

✰✰✰

"The Greatest Regimental Loss of the Entire War" went to The First Maine Heavy Artillery:  more than half of their 2,202 men were hit.

✰✰✰

*Only one war criminal was executed:  Henry Wirz,*
*the Commander of Andersonville Prison.*

✰✰✰

*The Cost of War for the U. S. Government was $2 million a day, amounting to $6 billion in all.  The South's total is estimated at $4 billion.*

✰✰✰

During the siege of Richmond by Grant, Lee's men (35,000 strong) were in desperate shape.  Firewood sold for $5. a stick; there were no rations, so they ate rats; boots sold for $300. a pair.  Flour was $400. a barrel and live chickens were $50.  Weakened as they were from lack of decent food, the Rebels faced 150,000 well-fed and well-armed Federals with 50,000 more men ready to call in Tennessee and the Shenandoah Valley.

✰✰✰

The term "sideburns" is a popular corruption of "burnsides", a style of side whiskers worn by and named for Union Major General Ambrose E. Burnside.

✰✰✰

*Abraham Lincoln had four brothers-in-law in the Confederate Army,
and three of his sisters-in-law were married to Confederate officers.*

The rugged McClellan saddle, designed by the Union
General himself, was the best of several types used in the
war.  An overcoat was strapped across the saddle bow,
a poncho and blanket across the cantle.

*The 8th Wisconsin Infantry had an eagle for a mascot.  "Old Abe"
was carried into battle at Vicksburg.  Soldiers reported that the bird
straightened and flapped its wings; then it flew low over the battlefield.*

☆☆☆

"The nature of the war placed a high premium on mobility.
Battles were won or lost on the ability of units to get into action
quickly.  In the 1862 Shenandoah Valley Campaign, Stonewall
Jackson's army of 16,000 tied up 63,000 Union troops and earned
the sobriquet "foot cavalry" by marching 600 miles in five weeks,
winning four battles along the way." (the Civil War Sourcebook)

☆☆☆

# What's in a Name?

The North called it "The War of the Rebellion".
The South liked "The War for Southern Independence".
Many just called it the "Civil War".
Some liked "The War Between the States."
Other monikers for this war were:

The War

The Late Unpleasantness

The Schism

The Uncivil War

The War for Constitutional Liberty

The Second American Revolution

The War for States' Rights

Mr. Lincoln's War

The Southern Rebellion

The War for Southern Rights

The War of the Southern Planters

The Second War for Independence

The War to Suppress Yankee Arrogance

The Brothers' War

The War of Secession

The Great Rebellion

The War for Nationality

The War for Southern Nationality

The War Against Slavery

The Civil War Between the States

The War of the Sixties

The War Against Northern Aggression

The Yankee Invasion

The War for Separation

The War for Abolition

The War for the Union

The Confederate War

The War of the Southrons

The War for Southern Freedom

The War of the North and South

The Lost Cause

# WAR WORDS

"America lives in the heart of every man everywhere who wishes to find a region where he will be free to work out his destiny as he chooses."

**-Woodrow Wilson**

⋆⋆⋆

**"With malice toward none; with charity for all;**
**with firmness in the right, as God gives us to see the right,**
**let us strive on to finish the work we are in;**
**to bind up the nation's wounds;**
**to care for him who shall have borne the battle,**
**and for his widow, and his orphan--**
**to do all which may achieve and cherish a just, and a lasting peace,**
**among ourselves, and with all nations."**

*-Abraham Lincoln, from his 2nd Inaugural address, 1865*

⋆⋆⋆

**"God grants liberty to those who love it, and are**
**always ready to guard and defend it."**

**-Daniel Webster**

⋆⋆⋆

*"A house divided against itself cannot stand."*

*-Abraham Lincoln*

⋆⋆⋆

"We have devoured the land and our animals
eat up the wheat and corn fields close.
All the people retire before us and desolation is behind.
To realize what war is, one should follow our tracks."

*-General William T. Sherman, on the campaign near Atlanta, 1864*

⋆⋆⋆

**"Go home, all you boys who fought with me,**
**and help to build up the shattered fortunes of our old state."**

*-Robert E. Lee in his address to his Confederate troops*
*after his surrender at Appomattox, April 9, 1865.*

⋆⋆⋆

*"And many are the dead men, too silent to be real."*

*-Gordon Lightfoot*

✫✫✫

**Man's "destiny is battle", said Oliver Wendell Holmes Jr.
Wounded three times in battle.**

✫✫✫

"The quickest way of ending a war is to lose it."

-George Orwell

✫✫✫

*"It is well that war is so terrible, or else we should grow too fond of it."*

*-Robert E. Lee*

✫✫✫

**"War is much too serious a matter to be entrusted to the military."**

-Georges Clemenceou

✫✫✫

"War is not good."

-Barbara Bush

✫✫✫

**"The real war will never get in the books."**

-Walt Whitman

✫✫✫

"Only the winners decide what were war crimes."

-Gary Wills

✫✫✫

*"In war there are no unwounded soldiers."*

*-Jose Narosky*

✫✫✫

*"Let every nation know, whether it wishes us
good or ill, that we will pay any price,
bear any burden, meet any hardship, support any friend, oppose any foe,
in order to assure the survival and the success of Liberty."*

*-John F. Kennedy, Inaugural Address, 1/20/61*

✫✫✫

*"Only our individual faith in freedom can keep us free."*

*-Dwight David Eisenhower*

★★★

*"I have never advocated war except as a means of peace."*

*-Ulysses S. Grant*

★★★

**"Fellow Citizens, we cannot escape history."**

*-Abe Lincoln*

★★★

*"America will never be destroyed from the outside.*
*If we falter and lose our freedoms it will be*
*because we destroyed ourselves."*

*-Abraham Lincoln*

★★★

**"Injustice anywhere is a threat to justice everywhere."**

*-Martin Luther King, Jr.*

★★★

*"For love of country they accepted death..."*

*-James A. Garfield*

★★★

*"It is easy to take liberty for granted, when you*
*have never had it taken from you."*

*-Vice President Dick Cheney*

★★★

**"Freedom is never free.  Where liberty dwells, there is my country."**

*-Ben Franklin*

★★★

America's first President and Commander-in-Chief, George
Washington, wrote that his most fervent wish was, "to see
this plague of mankind, war, banished from the earth."

★★★

*"All we ask is to be let alone."*

-Jefferson Davis, 1861

✶✶✶

*"Be sure you put your feet in the right place, then stand firm."*

*-Abe Lincoln*

✶✶✶

"Whoever saw a dead cavalryman?"

✶✶✶

*"I am tired and sick of war.  Its glory is all moonshine.*
*It is only those who have neither fired a shot nor heard*
*the shrieks and groans of the wounded, who cry aloud for*
*blood, more vengeance, more desolation.  War is hell."*
**--General William T. Sherman**
admonishing the graduating class of military cadets.
His advice for the growing hunger for war:  "suppress it."

✶✶✶

**"The war is over--the Rebels are our countrymen again."**

*-Ulysses S. Grant, after Lee's surrender;  April 9, 1865*

✶✶✶

**"War makes thieves and peace hangs them."**

**-George Herbert**

✶✶✶

**"Older men declare war but it is the youth who must fight and die."**

**-Herbert Hoover**

✶✶✶

## PICKETT'S CHARGE:
### (considered by many to be the most critical operation of the war)
"Only fifteen of the forty-six regiments that made the famous charge at Gettysburg were actually commanded by General Pickett, and of those, thirteen were led by Virginia Military School graduates, only two of whom survived the charge." When Lee chose Pickett's division to lead the attack on Cemetery Ridge, Pickett told his men, "Charge the enemy and remember old Virginia!" Pickett himself did not go, he and his aides watched from a nearby farm. *Less than half of Pickett's division returned from the ridge. He lost all of his regimental commanders and 16 out of 17 field officers under them. Later Lee ordered Pickett to prepare his division to repel a Union counterattack. "General Lee," Pickett replied, "I have no division now."* Pickett blamed Lee for the disastrous charge. Five years after the war, Pickett and Confederate guerrilla leader John Mosby visited Lee. Later, Pickett bitterly told Mosby, "That old man had my division slaughtered at Gettysburg." Mosby considered that for a moment before replying. "Well," said Mosby, "it made you immortal."

**"Anything worth dying for is worth living for."**

**-J. Heller**

★★★

**"You know the real meaning of PEACE only
if you have been through the war."**

**-Kosovar**

★★★

*"You win sometimes. I win sometimes. We're both Americans."*
*-Robert Redford, "Downhill Racer"*

★★★

**"Mankind must put an end to war, or war
will put an end to mankind."**

**-John F. Kennedy**

★★★

"A great war leaves the country with three armies,
an army of cripples, an army of mourners and an army of thieves."
-German proverb

★★★

"Everyone is a pacifist between wars.  It's like
being a vegetarian between meals."
-Coleman McCarthy

★★★

"In Flander's field the poppies grow
between the crosses, row on row
that mark our place, and in the sky the
larks, still bravely singing fly,
scarce heard amid the guns below."
-John McCrae

★★★

"War will exist until that distant day when the
conscientious objector enjoys the same reputation
and prestige that the warrior does today."
-J. F. Kennedy

★★★

"The pioneers of a warless world are the
youth that refuse military service."
-Albert Einstein

★★★

"A country cannot simultaneously prepare and prevent war."
-A. Einstein

★★★

*"I may be compelled to face danger, but
never fear it, and while our soldiers
can stand and fight, I can stand and feed and nurse them."*
*-Clara Barton*

★★★

*"Every gun that is made, every warship launched,*
*every rocket fired signifies, in the final sense,*
*a theft from those who hunger and are not fed,*
*those who are cold and not clothed."*

*-Dwight David Eisenhower*

★★★

**"They wrote in the old days that it is sweet**
**and fitting to die for one's country.**
**But in modern war there is nothing sweet nor fitting in your dying.**
**You will die like a dog for no good reason."**

**-Ernest Hemingway**

★★★

**"Never think that war, no matter how necessary,**
**nor how justified, is not a crime."**

**-Ernest Hemingway**

★★★

**"What difference does it make to the dead,**
**the orphans, and the homeless,**
**whether the mad destruction is wrought**
**under the name of totalitarianism**
**or the holy name of liberty and democracy."**

**-Ghandi**

★★★

*"Let loose the dogs of war."*

*-Marc Antony*

★★★

**"Freedom is the last, best hope on earth."**

-A. Lincoln

★★★

"We must be the great arsenal of Democracy."

-F.D. Roosevelt/Fireside Chat

★★★

*"There was never a good war or a bad peace."*

**-Ben Franklin**

★★★

*"Little girl...sometime they will give a war and nobody will come."*

-Carl Sandburg

★★★

**"Laws are silent in times of war."**

-Cicero

★★★

*"There is many a boy here today who looks on war as all glory,*

*but, boys, it is all HELL."*

-General William T. Sherman

★★★

*"We go forward to defend freedom and all*
*that is good and just in our world."*

-George W. Bush, President

★★★

The only U. S. Note to feature portraits of two presidents, Abraham Lincoln and Ulysses S. Grant, is the Black Eagle Dollar from 1899. Above the port, the majestic "Eagle of the Capital" spreads out its wings.   This bill is 1/3 larger than bills today.

# RALLY
# ROUND THE FLAG BOYS

Rally round the Flag Boys,
  Give it to the breeze,
That's the banner we love,
  On the land and seas;
Brave hearts are under it,
  Let the traitors brag,
Gallant boys, fire away,
  And fight for the Flag.

> Their flag is but a rag,
>   Ours is the true one,
> Up with the Stars and Stripes,
>   Down with the new one;
> Let our colors fly, boys,
>   Guard them day and night,
> For victory is liberty,
>   And God will bless the right.
>     Chorus.-Rally round, &c,

Floating high above us,
  Glowing in the sun,
Speaking loud to all hearts
  Of a freedom won.
Who dares to sully it?
  Bought with precious blood,
Gallant lads will fight for it,
  Tho' ours should swell the flood.

> Raise then the banner high,
>   Ours is the true one,
> Up with the Stars and Stripes,
>   Down with the new one;
> Let our colors fly boys,
>   Guard them day and night,
> For victory is Liberty,
>   And God will bless the right.
>     Chorus.-Rally round, &c.

"...It will be a glorious day for our country when all the children within its borders shall learn that the four years of fratricidal war between the North and the South was waged by neither with criminal or unworthy intent, but by both to protect what they conceived to be threatened rights and imperiled liberty: that the issues which divided the sections were born when the Republic was born, and were forever buried in an ocean of fraternal blood."

*--Lt. General John B. Gordon, CSA*

# Rally Round the Flag

Freedom is our birthright. But let us never forget that liberty comes with a price. American citizens have fought for our nation. Many have fought. Many have died. It is only right that we honor our veterans. We have the dashing General John "Black Jack" Logan (1826-1886) to thank for that. With his darkly handsome good looks, he was a dashing, brave, very popular man who was a prominent man in state politics (four times elected to the state legislature as a Democrat). He started the Grand Army of the Republic, a powerful Veterans' organization. He was a well-known Senator (twice in the United States Legislature) who went on to run for the Vice-Presidency. He then started Memorial Day, a day designed to have a nation stop and look back and be thankful for those who served in our military service…to give us pause to remember the lives sacrificed to keep our nation great. "Black Jack" Logan was known as the Nation's Greatest Volunteer, and the Best Volunteer General of the Civil War.

Our American flag has been the symbol of our country's unity and strength since its conception over 200 years ago. We look to our national colors with pride. Back in 1777 the Second Continental Congress adopted the stars and stripes of our American flag: thirteen stripes, alternating red and white, with thirteen stars, white in a blue field, representing a new constellation. The resolution did not specify arrangement of the stars, or the number of points. Some flag designs were scattered stars, while some flags arranged the stars in rows or circles. Some stars were six-pointed, some eight. There is strong evidence pointing to Francis Hopkinson of New Jersey being responsible for the inclusion of stars in the design. He was a signer of the *Declaration of Independence*.

It was President Monroe in 1818 who determined that the flag design would be changed on the next 4$^{th}$ of July following admission of any new states (stars were added). President Taft in 1912 set the size and proportions of the flag and determined that the point of the five point star went up. He also made the arrangement of the stars, which has been since changed twice by Executive Order, both times by President Eisenhower in January of 1959 and again in August of that year.

Today the flag has 50 stars for our 50 states, while the 13 stripes, seven red alternating with six white, represent America's 13 original colonies. The colors are symbolic: RED is for Hardiness and Valor; WHITE is for Purity and Innocence; BLUE symbolizes Vigilance, Perseverance and Justice.

The flags of the Civil War, both the Regimental and the Union and Confederate, were the pride of the army, summoning patriotism, love, loyalty, passion. The flag stood for the soldiers' bravery, a symbol of those who died protecting the flag. Many flags had been made by the women of the small towns, sent off to war with their men. Troops rallied to their flags. They followed their Color Bearer into battle, and they defended their flag to the death. The flag was used to communicate with the soldiers of the regiment, as the soldiers would look to their flag to know what to do: advance, retreat, or hold their ground.  A regiment was in disgrace if they lost their flag.  It was an honor to carry the flag, but the Color Guard had the most dangerous position.  The highest mortality rates of the war were suffered by the Color Bearers defending their flags in battle.  At Gettysburg the flag of the 24th Michigan was riddled with 23 bullets as nine Color Bearers died defending it as the regiment retreated, still fighting, from McPherson's Woods.

Most of the flags were made of silk, while some were wool or cotton bunting.  Many flags bear mottoes, especially the regimental original presentation flags.  The fringes are mostly silk floss, but some were "gold bullion", made with twisted gold-colored wire, particularly those from the famous New York jeweler Tiffany's.  The state of Michigan has 163 Civil War battle flags in the state collection.  The Battle Flag of the 1st Michigan Cavalry, Thomas Henry Sheppard's flag, is now in the Dearborn Museum in the Commandant's Quarters of the Detroit Arsenal at Dearbornville.  It is their most prized possession.

Flag Day began in 1916 when President Woodrow Wilson made a proclamation supporting the 1777 Flag Resolution that formally laid down the Stars and Stripes as American's symbol:  representing unity in diversity, one nation out of several.  Flag Day quietly reminds us all of flags unfurled; tattered, battle-worn flags displayed in museums; veterans' graves decorated for Memorial Day.  The flag is a talisman carried at home; a standard carried into battle; a gentle reminder of America's patriots.

Every time we see a tri-folded flag, we are immediately taken in our minds to the grave of a fallen soldier, the legacy of a warrior no longer with us.

And "Lest We Forget", despite the raging war going on all around, life still went on day to day throughout the rest of the Union and Confederacy. Tens of thousands of men dying at a time, and still the rest of life went on. A Thanksgiving proclamation from President Abraham Lincoln: "Done at the city of Washington this third day of October, in the year of our Lord one thousand eight hundred and sixty-three and of the Independence of the United States the eighty-eighth."

"The year that is drawing toward its close has been filled with the blessings of fruitful fields and healthful skies.  To these bounties, which are so constantly enjoyed that we are prone to forget the source from which they come, others have been added, which are of so extraordinary a nature that they cannot fail to penetrate and soften the heart which is habitually insensible to the ever-watchful providence of Almighty God.

"In the midst of a civil war of unequaled magnitude and severity... peace has been preserved with all nations, order has been maintained, the laws have been respected and obeyed, and harmony has prevailed everywhere, except in the theater of military conflict, while that theater has been greatly contracted by the advancing armies and navies of the Union.

"Needful diversions of wealth and strength from the fields of peaceful industry to the national defense have not arrested the plow, the shuttle or the ship; the ax has enlarged the borders of our settlements, and the mines, as well of iron and coal as of the precious metals, have yielded even more abundantly than heretofore. Population has steadily increased, notwithstanding the waste that has been made in the camp, the siege, and the battle-field and the country, rejoicing in the consciousness of augmented strength and vigor, is permitted to expect continuance of years with large increase of freedom.

"No human counsel hath devised, nor hath any mortal hand worked out these great things. They are the gracious gifts of the Most High God, who, while dealing with us in anger for our sins, hath nevertheless remembered mercy.

"It has seemed to me fit and proper that they should be solemnly, reverently, and gratefully acknowledged as with one heart and one voice by the whole American people. I do, therefore, invite my fellow-citizens in every part of the United States, and also those who are at sea and those who are sojourning in foreign lands, to set apart and observe the last Thursday of November next as a day of thanksgiving and praise to our beneficent Father who dwelleth in the heavens. And I recommend to them that, while offering up the ascriptions justly due to Him for such singular deliverances and blessings, they do also, with humble penitence for our national perverseness and disobedience, commend to His tender care all those who have become widows, orphans, mourners, or sufferers in the lamentable civil strife in which we are unavoidably engaged, and fervently implore the interposition of the Almighty hand to heal the wounds of the nation, and to restore it, as soon as may be consistent with the Divine purposes, to the full enjoyment of peace, harmony, tranquility, and union."

# WHY THE AMERICAN FLAG IS FOLDED 13 TIMES
## (from the US Air Force Academy)

*The 1st fold of our flag is a symbol of life.*

*The 2nd fold is a symbol of our belief in the eternal life.*

*The 3rd fold is made in honor and remembrance of the
veterans departing our ranks who gave
a portion of life for the defense of our country to
attain a peace throughout the world.*

*The 4th fold represents our weaker nature, for as American citizens trusting God,
it is to Him we turn to in times of peace as well as
in times of war for His divine guidance.*

*The 5th fold is a tribute to our country, for in the
words of Stephen Decatur, "Our Country,
in dealing with other countries may she always be right;
but it is still our country, right or wrong."*

*The 6th fold is for where our hearts lie. It is with our heart
that we pledge allegiance to the flag of the
United States of America, and to the republic for which it stands, one
nation, under God, indivisible, with liberty and justice for all.*

*The 7th fold is a tribute to our Armed Forces, for it is through the Armed
Forces that we protect our country and our flag against all her enemies,
whether they be found within or without the boundaries of our republic.*

*The 8th fold is a tribute to the one who entered into
the valley of the shadow of death,
that we might see the light of day, and to honor
mother for whom it flies on Mother's Day.*

*The 9th fold is a tribute to womanhood; for it had been
through their faith, love, loyalty and devotion
that the character of the men and women who have
made this country great has been molded.*

*The 10<sup>th</sup> fold is a tribute to father, for he, too, has given his sons and daughters*
*for the defense of our country since they were first born.*

*The 11<sup>th</sup> fold, in the eyes of a Hebrew citizen, represents*
*the lower portion of the seal of King David*
*and King Solomon, and glorifies in their eyes, the*
*God of Abraham, Isaac and Jacob.*

*The 12<sup>th</sup> fold, in the eyes of a Christian citizen, represents an emblem of eternity*
*and glorifies, in their eyes, God the Father, the Son and the Holy Spirit.*

*When the flag is completely folded, the stars are uppermost,*
*reminding us of our nation's motto, "In God We Trust."*

*After the flag is completely folded and tucked in, it takes on the*
*appearance of a cocked hat, ever reminding us of the soldiers who*
*served under General George Washington and the sailors and marines*
*who served under Captain John Paul Jones who were followed by their*
*comrades and shipmates in the Armed Forces of the United States,*
*preserving for us the rights, privileges, and freedoms we enjoy today.*

Thomas Henry Sheppard

# HE KEPT THE COLORS

The true story of

# THE GENERAL, THE OLD MAN AND THE FLAG

A factual account from Marlette, Michigan, the Heart of the Thumb

*"He who is guided by love of country is guarded by God."*
*- L . E. J.*

This is a love story,
the very greatest kind of love
that some in this country will never understand.
It is the love and deepest respect
a man has for his country
and for his President and Commander-In-Chief.
It is a story of heroes,
for every single person who ever went
off to war in America's name
or to serve his country is one of America's heroes…
Never forget,

*"All gave some, and Some gave all."*

# Prologue:

*September 13, 1884*
*Marlette, Michigan*


"Then the train moved on, and the last thing General Logan and I saw was the old man standing there with his flag."


-- William Bates, aide to General John A. (Black Jack) Logan regarding their trip across Michigan in Logan's whistle-stop campaign for the Vice-Presidency of the United States.
*(Marlette Leader, Detroit Journal)*

# He Kept the Colors

*\*\* This is a war story which may well give a different viewpoint of war-- it is a story of complete and absolute patriotism, of love of country, of one man's love and respect for his country. It tells briefly of Michigan county regiments through the war...then it accompanies other Michigan men... stories that are often lost in the bigger story of war. Lastly, it follows one Michigan man and the flag he carried.*

## The Military Beginnings of
## Sanilac County & the Thumb of Michigan

War is no stranger to the great state of Michigan. Military battlefields dot the Southern part of Michigan from the War of 1812. Michigan likewise furnished a goodly number of gentlemen (and otherwise) to bear arms for the Black Hawk War. The Peninsula State was also well represented in the War with Mexico. But it has been said, "No human voice responded to any of these calls to arms from the lonely forests of 'The Thumb'". Dense forestlands almost totally covered the area even in 1861, leaving virtually no settlements here at that time.

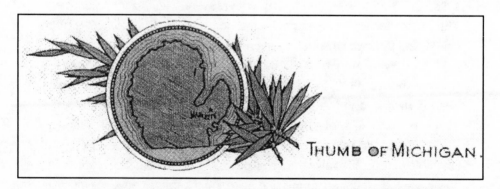

THUMB OF MICHIGAN

Michigan's lovely 'Thumb', itself a peninsula among peninsulas, was "lulled in the cradle of peace". Hunting was about the only time gunshots were ever heard, until the awful suddenness of the Civil War rocked the entire state of Michigan with a call for men and arms. The shocking news of the firing of Sumter brought the men to their feet, and news of the Battle of Bull Run pushed patriotism to the forefront.

It is said that when the call for volunteers came out from President Lincoln, the response from all over the Union was joined with voices from Sanilac County shouting, "We are coming, Father Abraham, three hundred thousand more!"

The first to answer the call militarily from the Thumb in November of 1861 were the 'Sanilac Wolverines', an elite fighting group soon known militarily as 'Co. D, 10ᵗʰ Michigan Infantry'. A few brave volunteers had previously joined the Second and the Seventh regiments. Company D gathered under the able leadership of Capt. Israel Hucking, who raised about sixty of our best citizens. The 'Wolverines' set forth for battle on Tuesday, November 19, 1861.

Their tale is most eloquently told by the Chapman Brothers, <u>1884</u> <u>*Album of Sanilac County*</u>: "The company took passage on the 'Forester' for Flint, the rendezvous for the regiment, and were enrolled as Company D of the 10ᵗʰ Michigan Infantry. The night was dark and windy,--ominous of the stormy times through which the boys were to pass,--yet there were very large numbers of citizens from all parts of the county down to the dock in Lexington to see the 'Forester' swing off with her load of brave men on a journey from which there was such uncertain return, and to add a 'God-Bless-You', and perhaps a last 'Good-bye!' As the last rope was pulled in, three times three hearty cheers were given to those on deck, who responded with a prolonged hurrah for the flag. The boys left in good spirits, and thus was the inauguration of the war in Sanilac County."

By January of 1862, their company quota was filled. They left Flint on April 22, 1862, for Pittsburg Landing with a full roster of 103 men. They participated in the following events: the evacuation of Corinth; a march to Tuscumbia, Alabama, to guard the railroad and the river landing at Florence on the Tennessee River; besiegement under General Palmer at Nashville until the arrival of the Army of the Cumberland under Rosecrans; 18 were killed, wounded, or missing guarding the trains between Nashville and Murfreesboro. At that point, they spent three months in Nashville, until July of 1863, and their gentlemanly conduct and faithful discharge of duty won for them the admiration and esteem of the local citizenry. The good manners and quiet respect shown by the Michigan regiment caused a very large number of the people of Nashville to sign a petition asking that the Michigan men be allowed to remain as guards. This petition was presented to General Rosecrans, who, although impressed, could not grant the petition. Thus, the regiment moved on to Murfreesboro.

Again according to the Chapman Brothers' historical account, from there the Michigan regiment went on to Stevenson, Alabama, and then into the Sequachee Valley, thence continuing over Waldron's Ridge to Smith's Ferry on the Tennessee River. As the battle of Mission Ridge was beginning, the 10th Michigan Wolverines were pulled out and placed temporarily under the command of General Sherman, who held them in reserve during Mission Ridge, then going after the enemy and driving them out of Chickamauga the following morning. They continued with General Sherman's forces to Knoxville, then back again to Chattanooga, <u>marching 24 days on five days' rations</u>! They were mustered as a veteran regiment, but before receiving their furlough, they were engaged at Buzzard's Roost, Georgia, and lost about 70 men killed, wounded and prisoners. Of the 15 prisoners, only two ever returned, the rest were starved to death in rebel prisons.

From the Louisville *Journal*, "with their furloughs in their pockets, and preparations made to visit their dear ones at home from whom they had been parted so long, the bugles on the 25th of the month just passed found the 10th Michigan responsive, with flags unfurled, and on the march for the battlefield. They fought with the 60th Illinois under Morgan at Buzzard's Roost, with the menacing Rocky Face looming above. Charging through a deadly fire of artillery, with the infantry carrying their colors to the enemy's very works, the 10th Michigan lost much more than the 25 patriots killed and wounded, for among their dead lay the body of their own Lieutenant Colonel Dickerson."

After returning from furlough with a number of badly needed new Michigan recruits, the 10th rejoined their brigade in Georgia, at a place called Resaca, from whence they went on to Rome to help in its capture. They then remained with Sherman's army throughout the march that resulted in the capture of Atlanta, with both their courage and endurance duly noted. They lost 21 men, six from Company D, at Peach-Tree Creek on July 20, 1864. Later on in Jonesboro on the 1st of September, they lost

77 more dead, and many soldiers so badly wounded that they would soon succumb, among them Captain H. H. Nims of D Company, who died the following day. The captain's death dealt the Michigan men a tough blow, for Nims was much loved by all who knew him, both on the field and back in the heart of Sanilac County.

1864 was the worst year, with over 200 killed, wounded or missing. The Wolverines, as a matter of record, lived up to their name by snapping at the heels of Nathan Forrest through Athens, Georgia, by railroad, then on to Florence. Back to Chattanooga, the Wolverines continued on after Hood as they chased him into Alabama. At this point, the 10th Michigan marched on with General Sherman right into the streets of Savannah. Many men of the 10th were lost at the Battle of Bentonville. History records that the Michigan brigade's legendary bravery and determination circumvented a disaster there that day.

The 10th participated in Washington at the Grand Review on May 24, 1865, and they were mustered out of service in July, paid off and disbanded by August back in Jackson, Michigan. Total roll call: 1,788 men and officers. The losses totaled 299.

When the call went out in July of 1862 for more volunteers, another company from Sanilac County was formed: Company K, which joined the 22nd, now consisting of 997 men. The flag they carried was given to the regiment by the young ladies of Pontiac, and the flag was defended to the very last at Chickamauga. At this place, practically the entire regiment was taken prisoner, killed, or wounded, while the three color-bearers were severely wounded. The regiment spent most of its time from April 14 to September 5 doing "interior" duty in Nashville. They moved by rail 122 miles to Bridgeport, Alabama, crossing in pontoons and camping on islands, until they joined General Thomas at Chickamauga as reinforcements. Colonel LeFavour said, regarding the conduct of the 22nd Michigan, "at the second charge the rebels drove the brigade to the bottom of the hill. It was reformed, marched up, and again took the crest. The regiment was out of ammunition and word was sent to General Whittaker to that effect." "You must use your steel", was the reply. The regiment rushed forward with fixed bayonets and empty muskets under a terrific fire of grape and musketry, received the countercharge of the enemy, repulsed and drove at them at every point. But alas, their gallantry was their disaster! So eager were they, they came out far in advance of the others, and when the call came to fall back, it was too late! Darkness was their friend, but the delay had allowed the enemy to close in, and only a few had escaped, with the rest of the living made prisoners, the others all dead on the field.

A young Union drummer boy named Johnny Clem ran away to war before he was ten years old. He marched with the 22nd Michigan Regiment to major battles, including Murfreesboro, Atlanta, and Shiloh. His claim to fame came at the battle of Chickamauga in Tennessee. When a Confederate officer galloped towards him shouting, "Surrender, you little devil!", Clem shot him with a musket that had been sawed off to fit him, and the wounded officer was taken prisoner.

The Wolverines who had managed to survive thus far now spent some time digging and building fortifications and doing picket duty along the Tennessee River. Then they moved to support General Hooker in the south of Tennessee.

For the remainder of the war, the Michiganders were attached mainly to the Engineer Brigade, under General William F. Smith, and those of the Huron Peninsula were commended for their march through Kentucky over bad roads, through rain and snow, but *"as they have always done, discharged their duty faithfully!"* They worked in the engineer brigade building roads, repairing railroads and bridges up and down the Tennessee River, until they went with Sherman to Atlanta. They were then detailed as escort to the headquarters of Major-General Thomas. They were mustered out on June 20, 1865, and arrived in Detroit to be paid off and discharged on July 11.

From a roll of 1,586 men, 374 men died of disease, including 3 officers; 53 men were killed in action, one an officer, and 27 men and 2 officers died of wounds.

Sanilac County also provided some men for the 6th Michigan Cavalry, which was organized at Grand Rapids. They sent 1,229 men and officers into battle, carrying a flag given to them by Gen. James H. Kidd in 1863. At the end of the war, this regiment went to Wyoming to battle Indians, and this same flag was the first to fly over Fort Reno on the Powder River. Their numbers included 102 men and officers killed; 18 dead of wounds; 266 dead from disease.

A few men of the county went into the 24$^{th}$, 27$^{th}$, 8$^{th}$, and 14$^{th}$ Infantries, and like all of the brave men of Sanilac County, our sons can all be looked upon with pride and honor, for their steadfastness and bravery. In time of need, Sanilac County responded nobly to the call.

Lest we forget the ladies of the county, they immediately offered their able assistance to the war effort, forming a Soldiers' Relief Society at Lexington, and a Soldiers' Aid Society at Port Sanilac. Many were the boxes of shirts, dried and preserved fruits, newspapers, socks, handkerchiefs, blankets, bandages, knick-knacks, magazines, and other necessities that were sent by our women to the hospitals and camps of our Michiganders. (Unfortunately, it was later found out that the boxes sent South to the prison camps went mainly to the officers and soldiers of the Confederacy). All Sanilac soldiers deserve a hearty approval for their courage in time of war.

## The Rest of the Story of
## Sanilac County and the Thumb of Michigan
*Taken from the 1884 story told by Chapman Brothers*

One seldom-told aspect of the war can be told here, taken from county records. It seems that local men, wishing to be trained and ready to take to the field whenever their Commander-In-Chief called, formed companies in both Lexington and also Davisville (now Croswell) for the purpose of concentrated military drill and training. The two companies met weekly and daily for drill, and apparently did so for some considerable length of time, just waiting to be called. Had this been initiated at the war's beginning, it is thought that much of the large amounts of treasure and many lives might have been saved. Whoever would have thought that war would or could start so suddenly? Or would go on for so long and be so bloody? They had no media to trumpet the violence and enumerate the casualty lists every evening in the nightly news.

In the words of the Chapman Brothers, "Only the cold facts that a part of the country had rebelled, and hundreds of lives had been lost without effect, could inform a war-hating people that the monster was upon them, for few of them knew anything of active service, and civil hostilities indeed seemed to have no place on the American continent. Yet the stranger knocked at an unsuspected time, and the oil in Uncle Sam's lamp was low."

Irregardless of all this, Sanilac stepped up to the plate when the call came loud and clear for help. The county responded quickly with more than their fair share in supplies and aid, and the required draft requests. At this point in time, Sanilac County was covered almost entirely with pine trees, and the population was scarce. Only 40 men were conscripted, as they required only 238, and more than 200 soldiers had already volunteered. As it turned out, no drawing was necessary, as the courageous volunteers had already surpassed the draft amount. However, the brave men put to shame the cowards who ran into hiding in Canada or slipped into the dense woods nearby to avoid the draft.

Close at hand and to the north of Sanilac, comprising the tip of Michigan's Thumb, lay Huron County. An interesting story emerged from Huron at that same time, a tale that caused much excitement and righteous indignation along the entire lakeshore. It had the making of a potentially serious disturbance. It was January of 1865, and a company of 75 men, uniformed and disciplined soldiers, were hot on the trail of what everyone assumed might possibly turn into a fiery conflagration. Armed and carrying rations for ten days, the men were marching to aid County Treasurer Cottrell and Sheriff Mankin who had run into trouble after taking by force two drafted Polanders who were not ready to serve in the War. The officers left Paris Township in Huron County when they were surrounded by roughly 30 armed men, mostly Polanders themselves, led by Francis Talaga, demanding they give up the drafted men. With loaded rifles pointed at the officers' heads, surrender was the only option. However, the rioters were totally enraged, and they began firing at the county officers, with bullets just barely missing their heads. "The foreigners, ignorant of our laws and customs, had in all probability been incited to the attack by the pestilential peace-makers who opposed the war."

This incident led many to believe that an uprising was imminent, thus precipitating the arrival of the armed soldiers marching along the shoreline of the Thumb. On the 15th of January, 1865, expecting trouble from a determined and desperate band of hostiles, the soldiers found no resistance anywhere, and the hostile band of desperadoes were peaceably going about their daily business.

Another story of praise for the women of the county and the country is found in a letter written by a soldier under General Rosecrans in West Virginia, from which an excerpt is taken: "...my system finally gave way to the fever which had been sapping its strength for weeks, and an ambulance bore me to the hospital. Under the care of our skillful regimental surgeon, Dr. Salter, the fever was broken in a week...My hospital life was far more pleasant than I anticipated. Up among the mountains, entering a hospital was equivalent to speaking for a coffin. Hence all made an effort to keep on duty, in order to keep out of the hospital. But it is not so bad at the post hospital at Charleston. Large, commodious buildings are used as an abode for the sick, and the comforts of the Ladies' Aid Society do much to prepare the soldier again for duty. BLESS THEIR SOULS! I well remember that, after lying with my knapsack for a pillow, my head almost bursting with pain, when I was removed to another ward and supplied with quilts, coverlets, feather pillows, sheets and pillow slips by their fair hands, and my head resting upon the soft, soothing pillow,--I could not help it--my eyes closed and I thank God that our country has such women."

*"Men of the silent bands,*
*Men of half-told days,*
*Lift up your specter hands*
*And take our sweet bouquets."*

*- Will Carleton*

# The Michigan Cavalry Brigade Monument in Gettysburg:

*But foremost in the fight you'll see*
*Where'er the bravest dare be,*
*The sabres of thy cavalry*
*Michigan, my Michigan*

## 1861 - MICHIGAN and the CIVIL WAR

Michigan's belief in the integrity of the Union was mainly what led 12% of its population to go off to war, with 802 battles and skirmishes to her credit. *LEST WE FORGET*, Michigan had 14,855 graves filled when war was done. To say Michigan did her part for the war is a vast understatement. Her involvement was universal. Michigan was represented when Confederate shelling of Fort Sumter on April 12, 1861, started the Civil War, in the form of Michigan Second Lieutenant Norman J. Hall of the 1st U.S. Artillery. On May 16 the first Western regiment to reach the Capital after Abe's call for troops to defend it were the soldierly-looking Michigan troops as they arrived in Washington at 10 p.m. and were warmly welcomed. Hundreds of people came out to greet them, as well as a band, preceding them across town past the White House, causing Honest Abe to say, "Thank God for Michigan!" Likewise, on the day Robert E. Lee and his men met General Grant in final surrender at Appomattox, the Peninsula State was also represented there by the 16th and the 1st Michigan Volunteer Infantry regiments who received the Confederate troops. And when the Union's beloved President Lincoln was assassinated, it was a Michigan regiment who had the distinct honor of accompanying his casket back to Springfield for burial. Michigan units quickly joined in the hunt for John Wilkes Booth, the accused killer of Lincoln. When Jefferson Davis fled after the Confederacy fell, it was the Michigan Cavalry who rounded him up.

In addition to these facts, Frank Woodford's delightful book, <u>Father Abraham's Children</u>, also relates that fifty soldiers from Michigan earned the Congressional Medal of Honor for their efforts in the Civil War. Michigan also supplied much of the meat for the soldiers, as well as many of the horses for the cavalry.

# HE KEPT THE COLORS

*This is the true story of Thomas Henry Sheppard, Color Sergeant, Company E, 1st Michigan Cavalry. Thomas' story is somewhat different from that of his closest neighbors in Sanilac County, for he did not wait to join the Wolverines in the Infantry, but rather went right into the 1st Michigan Cavalry*

*several months earlier. He was still a Michigan Wolverine, nonetheless! And his "Colors" were always and ever his pride and delight. The bit of red, white and blue bunting with its 34 stars, so very stunningly beautiful as Thomas headed off to war, soon would become worn and tattered, riddled with many bullets and saber tears, faded by the sun and rain of many killing fields...and with every strike against it, the old flag took on an even greater beauty, filled with dignity and the deepest respect. The "Colors" have an interest in their own right to every man, woman and child in America, in the past, now and always.*

The rank of Color Bearer was a great honor, given to a carefully chosen patriot who had shown the utmost in courage. It was basically one of the most dangerous positions in the entire regiment, as the Color Bearer was usually unarmed in battle, carrying nothing but his flag, Union or regimental. Thomas did not carry the regimental flag. He proudly held the Union flag of 34 stars, made for him before he left for the war...four stately rows of eight stars with an additional star between each two rows. That flag was held aloft in battle, and the men of the regiment rallied round their flag during every fierce battle. The flag stood for much more than words can say--it stood for God and country, for the beautiful mountains, the calm and the turbulent oceans, the wide windy prairies--those "broad stripes and bright stars" really stood for everything that was good in America.

From an interview Thomas gave in the Detroit Free Press when he was on his way back to Gettysburg after the war for a reunion: "(Thomas) took the colors from the camp at Hamtramck and carried them to the front with his regiment. The men saw hot service, and many of them, including the gallant colonel (Brodhead), never came back. They fought through the Shenandoah, on Banks' advance and retreat, in the campaigns of Pope and Burnside, and did yeoman service at the battle of Gettysburg. They were under fire up to May 1863, twice at Winchester, at Middletown, Strasburg, Harrisonburg, Orange Court House, Cedar Mountain, the second Bull Run, Occoquan and Thoroughfare Gap".

This precious flag had literally been through the war.

# THOMAS IN THE BEGINNING

Thomas Henry Sheppard was a native of Bristol, England. The United States was the melting pot of humanity in the mid-1800's, when the land of opportunity gladly took in 4,500,000 immigrants between 1840 and 1860. Almost half of these were Irish and German, while the rest were English, Scottish, and Scotch-Irish.

Bristol, located on the Irish Sea, was an important shipping port. Their boys almost always followed tradition and went to sea. Thomas, born April 4, 1822, to Mary Ann Hill and William Sheppard, was no exception. Blue-eyed and fair-haired, Thomas was about 5'7" tall. He sailed merchant ships over the Irish Sea to Ireland and over the English Channel to Europe. He married Louisa Umphrey on July 19, 1840, and settled down into the carpenter trade. Five children were born in England when Thomas decided to come to America in 1853.

After finding work in New York, Thomas sent for his family. Louisa, pregnant with her sixth child, and with five in tow, boarded a sailing ship for America. After a long and arduous journey was almost over, the winds changed and the sailing ship was blown back almost to England. Thomas must have been a good provider, for the expense of tickets for such a large family would not have been cheap. They settled in New York, at a place called Bird's Eye. Thomas once again sailed the merchant ships, only this time on the Great Lakes. He also did surveying work, while farming and making bricks. They moved to Detroit, then north to Michigan's Thumb near Almont.

★★★

"Americans are seldom prepared for their wars when they erupt, and the Civil War was no exception." "...a sad group of old friends gathered for the last time...to bid farewell to half a dozen of their number who were about to embark upon an overland journey to the new Confederacy...as tears welled in the eyes of all present, hearts...were filled with sadness over the sundering of life-long ties, and doubts to the result of their sacrifice." As the group broke up, one man wept openly, saying "You can never know what this has cost me." "Praying that he might be struck dead rather than have to fight his old friends, he and the others rode off..." (Commanders of the Civil War) It was a scene oft-repeated from ocean to ocean, the devastating thoughts of fighting against their friends.

Trouble had definitely been brewing for some time when the first gun was fired the morning of April 12, 1861, by the Confederates of South Carolina onto Fort Sumter in the Charleston Harbor. It was to change America forever. Many great leaders would find themselves on both sides of this disturbing conflict. Also, many very good men but very bad leaders…the war brought out the best in men and the worst in men.

It took only 34 hours for Fort Sumter, federally held, to surrender. President Lincoln quickly called for volunteers in his efforts to preserve the Union. Michigan was quick to react, as the men could do little but talk about war and the "Northern Cause". Enlistment was the main thought in the days after Sumter. It was a bit frenzied, and the romance of war was in the air. Little did they know how disappointing the real thing would be.

By May 23, the state of Virginia had seceded, making Richmond the new capital of the new Confederacy. Richmond naturally became the Union's main target. The 1st Battle of Manassas near Bull Run River was the resulting clash of Maj. General McDowell's Federal army of 35,000 men advancing, preparing to cross the Potomac to take Richmond after first capturing the Manassas Gap Railroad and the Orange & Alexandria Railroad. Beauregard, the Confederate General, placed his 32,000 recruits at the junction waiting for the federals. Despite battling back and forth all day under the sweltering July 21st sun, with a heavy casualty list on both sides and plenty of observers enjoying their picnic lunch while viewing the festivities, no apparent winner surfaced until late in the day. Then the Union forces beat a hasty disorganized retreat back to Washington, only 25 miles to the north, followed closely by the partying crowd. No one could believe that the Rebels had beaten the Union in their first big fight! President Lincoln resolved to arm for full war and replaced General McDowell with General McClellan as commander. Recruiting began in earnest all over the Ohio Valley, the Great Lakes, and out East. Meanwhile, the picnickers readied themselves for what they hoped would be another day of fun.

The newly formed First Michigan Volunteer Cavalry Regiment took men who wanted to fight for their country. Some had no sympathy for the South or for slavery. Others opposed tearing the Union apart. Still others went simply because the bounty for joining was considerable. Thomas Henry Sheppard, husband of Louisa, now father of eight children (Ella, Henry, Louisa, Frederick George, Selina, Charles Benjamin, Theodore,

William) apparently joined for all of these reasons, signing with the 1st Michigan for a three year enlistment, assigned initially to Company L. Louisa, his wife, argued long and strong for Thomas not to go to war. What on earth would she do with a farm and eight children? But Thomas loved his country and his president, and when President Lincoln called for volunteers, Thomas was one of the first to go. The women of the Marlette area, just to the north of Sheppard's home, made the 34-star American flag for Thomas to carry.

By August 21 of 1861 the crops were mostly in on his small farm in the Thumb of Michigan when Thomas left by train from Almont for Detroit. He had packed a small leather bag, and carrying his precious Union flag, departed with well-wishes and cheers. Louisa cried her eyes out.

From Detroit he was sent to Hamtramck, where he was mustered in at Camp Lyon into Company L, 1st Brigade, 1st Division of the First Michigan Cavalry. Their commanding officer was Colonel Thornton Franklin Brodhead, who had just resigned as Postmaster of Detroit to accept the appointment as Commanding Officer of the 1st Michigan. Before the men left, they were all fitted for uniforms and arms from the Detroit Arsenal.

Springwells citizens presented a regimental flag for the First to carry. Made of blue silk and fringed all around, it bore the national arms on both sides, with "First Michigan Cavalry" emblazoned below. The regimental flag was as beautiful in its own way as the magnificent Stars and Stripes that Thomas was to carry. "Old Glory" is what they called her.

The United States Military Reserve and Detroit Arsenal at Dearbornville was constructed in 1833. It has proudly served the people of the United States since then in many ways. U. S. Army Lieutenant Joshua Howard was in charge of the military storehouse and weapons repair shop. The arsenal was not small nor insignificant, nor was it fortified for defense. A brick wall and gates surrounded the beautiful parade grounds.

Eleven buildings made up the Detroit Arsenal. The powder magazine was to the east of the arsenal, a one story building with walls two feet thick, which was used for the storage of explosive ammunition and gunpowder. The magazine was located such that if it exploded, it would not destroy the entire arsenal. Below that ran the Rouge River, where a dock allowed heavy loads to be brought in when the water was high.

The United States Military Reserve surrounded the installation. It was made up of an immense amount of land comprising water, grasslands and lumber. North of the arsenal on the flood plains of the Rouge River there were barns, stables and pastureland. This area in 2006 is Ford Field and beyond. They used the lumber off the grounds for the needs of the military. The wood was for the buildings and for gun carriages and ships.

During the Civil War in 1864, the military storekeeper of the arsenal was a Mr. Charles Wilkins. He was on active duty from the U.S. Army Ordnance Department, a civilian with no official army rank, but paid as a captain. Helping him were eight other men who were also from the Ordnance Department, on duty...six privates, one corporal and one sergeant of ordnance. Sgt. John S. Cosbey had risen through the military ranks over a period of time spent at the Detroit Arsenal. It was his job to catalogue and store all of the arsenal weapons, from cavalry swords to big artillery, as well as tracking the used weapons through the reconditioning process.

The Veteran Reserve Corps served at the Arsenal as guards. They also were sent to escort supply wagons from the arsenal back to the field. The Corps consisted of soldiers wounded in combat, ill or for whatever reason not able to serve at the front. In contrast to the dark blue uniforms worn by the Union men, these soldiers wore light blue uniforms. During the Civil War, Company F, 2nd Regiment under Capt. Davenport served the arsenal.

Other uses of the Detroit Arsenal during the Civil War included hospital duty. For example, troops of the 21st Michigan stopped at the arsenal to get ordnance supplies and ammunition. They would bivouac inside the military reserve, while the surgeon, Dr. Edward Snow of Dearbornville, the acting Army Surgeon, would operate on the wounded men.

The men of Thomas Henry Sheppard's new military family, the 1st Michigan Volunteer Corps, left for the war on the 29th of September carrying new weapons and ammunition from the Detroit Arsenal at Dearbornville. Now, these men were mainly shop hands, lumberjacks and farm boys. They were mostly boys and young men. Thomas Henry was the exception. He was 39 years old. When the 1150 men were all in place, fired up and ready to go, the exuberant group of would-be soldiers left by train, flags waving and people cheering, to join other new recruits at their new training camp at Camp Frederick, Maryland.

The new camp was located about 50 miles northwest of Washington. It was to be their temporary home for most of the winter, with its main job the defense of the Upper Potomac River, the Shenandoah Valley, and the Eastern Blue Ridge Mountains. Not much was going on there, so mostly they spent hour after hour learning how to shoot their new weapons and drill, drill, drill. Rifle marksmanship, basic military training, horsemanship, teamwork, formations, commands were all part of the intensive training they underwent. They had to learn how to live in a tent city, work together as soldiers, and in general, fuse as an armed unit. They were "The Army of the Potomac for the Defense of the Capital".

Thomas Henry Sheppard advanced quickly from Private to Sergeant, was transferred from Company L to Company E, and was named Color Bearer for his new company. The army still spent its days in intensive training. It wasn't all work and no play, however. The realities of war had not yet set in, and they spent many hours telling stories and singing around the campfire.

During lulls in the war activity, Thomas accompanied Colonel Thornton Brodhead back to Michigan to enlist recruits. It was fairly quiet in the early days, and the time passed quickly enough until the spring of 1862, when the troops were placed under the command of Major General Nathanial P. Banks, a former Governor of Massachusetts, a 10-year Congressman, and a staunch Republican Party member and organizer. Banks was a thin man and quite tall. His handlebar mustache set him apart from the rest in looks. He was brave, courageous and bold, it seems, but he was definitely not a man with military wisdom or expertise. His job was to guard the Potomac from Washington City all the way to Manassas Junction. The rail line at Manassas needed some major repairs, causing the Confederates to leave the area.

At about that same time, while Thomas Henry Sheppard was in training at Camp Frederick, the South was also preparing for accelerated war. Robert E. Lee resigned his West Point commission early in the Civil War to take over the Confederate command. Both of these commanders, Lee and Banks, knew well the importance of the Shenandoah Valley and who would control it. General Lee looked to a veteran of the Mexican War to spearhead the Shenandoah campaign and to guard the valley. Lieutenant General Thomas J. Jackson was his man. Jackson had shown himself well at First Manassas, and the troops had taken to calling him "Stonewall" after an incident there. Others continued to call him "Old Jack". A large man, at least six feet tall, he had a full beard and curly brown hair, belying his uncompromising manner. While demanding the best of every man in his command, he spoke little, riding a diminutive horse he called "Little Sorrel", presenting a somewhat incongruous picture for anyone who saw him.

The Shenandoah Valley, 165 miles long, was one of the loveliest places anywhere on earth. It was named after the Shenandoah River. The river ran all the way from Harper's Ferry in the north where it flows into the Potomac River down to Lexington. Its eastern side was the beautiful Blue Ridge Mountain Range, while its west side was the equally lovely Allegheny Mountains. Nearly all of the eastern states and Virginia depended on the Shenandoah Valley for the main part of their food supply. If the Confederacy was to succeed, it must have the food from the Valley-- beef, grain and fruits. Stonewall Jackson said, "If this Valley is lost, Virginia is lost." It became the central part of their military strategy.

Likewise, it was the main objective of General Banks and his Army of the Potomac, a force of 18,000 freshly trained Federals. It was early in the spring of 1862. Their mission was to cross the Potomac River at Harper's Ferry and chase that devil of a commander, Stonewall Jackson.

Thomas Henry Sheppard proudly carried the flag of 34 stars that had been given to him before he left for the war. Color bearers are non-combatants, with his job keeping the Union flag he was responsible for aloft whenever the regiment was moving. The beautiful flag was huge, bright, fresh in color and sound throughout. It was Thomas' pride and joy, and for the duration of the war, it was his life. As they crossed the Potomac and rode through the place called Harper's Ferry and on into Charleston, his commander, Colonel Brodhead, ordered Thomas to hang their Union beauty from the window of the Courthouse at Charleston. It was their way of saying, "So there!" Alas, the proud women of Charleston, their men off to war elsewhere, made the strikingly handsome flag their target, and when the 1st Michigan moved on, taking down their flag as they left Charleston, it was no longer whole, the virgin flag having taken five bullet holes to "show the feelings of the irreconcilables in petticoats." (Thomas' words, interview in *Detroit Free Press*). One might say the women of Charleston were a bit rude--while others might think them darn unfriendly to the boys in blue. They were definitely determinedly hostile to the handsome Union men. This precious flag was to receive many more bullet and saber holes, some from just about each confrontation yet ahead, as it was proudly carried aloft in this War Between the States.

Thomas Henry was assigned not only to be the Color Bearer for the 1st Michigan, but the Sergeant was also a trusted dispatch carrier and scout during "down times". It appears that it must have been while he was out on his own carrying messages and scouting around that he first met up with a man who was to become famous along with his brother, Jesse, at a later point in time. Frank James had performed the similar service of scouting for the Confederate Army both before and during his days as a member of Quantrill's famous Raiders. As soon as his age would allow, Frank's younger brother joined him. The Civil War was considered a "Gentlemen's War", and scouts and dispatchers at times met up with their opposites and treated each other courteously.

Mr. Sheppard spoke often of the famous James brothers after he was back on the farm in Michigan, so he must have known them fairly well and respected them. It must have come as quite a surprise to him when he first realized it was his old acquaintances who were being written about in the newspapers so often after the war ended. Thomas must have especially enjoyed hearing the story of the Widow and the Mortgage. (Paul Harvey's The Rest of the Story). *It seems that three men, tired and hungry, far from home, stopped at a house along their route. When the lady of the house came out, the gentlemen asked her if by any chance they might be able to get a home-cooked meal, as they were long on the trail. She replied that she had little, but what she had she would gladly share with them. They sat down to a tasty noon meal. They could tell that she was*

51

*very poor. One of the men noticed a tear running down the woman's cheek. He asked her what was wrong. She replied that it had been a long time since she had men at her table, and it just made her sad. Her husband had died a year ago. Oh, and there was something else, too. This very day the man who held the mortgage on her property was coming at 4:00 p.m. to foreclose. She just didn't have the money, what with her husband dead and all. They asked her how much, and she replied $800.--a hundred times more than she could ever come up with. The men felt terrible that they had imposed on her, and soon got up to leave. As they mounted their horses, one man reached down to shake the widow's hand. Into her hand he pressed a wad of bills...currency...$800. "You get a receipt now, you hear?" This is just one of the many stories Thomas heard about his old friends, Frank and Jesse James. This one actually happened, in the 1870's in the gentle Ozark Mountain foothills. Oh, by the way, when the man who held the widow's mortgage had departed her house after receiving her mortgage money, paid in full...he was robbed in the woods nearby...he was robbed of all the money he was carrying, including the widow's mortgage money...he was robbed by the "stranger", the "mysterious benefactor"... Jesse James.*

The war began to pick up around the time of the Shenandoah Campaign. It must have been quite a sight to see as General Banks and his entourage on horseback left Charleston and moved slowly southward up the Shenandoah Valley. The supply wagons were loaded to the max, pulled by horses and accompanied by 80 cannon and around two thousand men on horseback. The Cavalry itself was polished and poised, moving as they were towards Winchester, General Jackson's headquarters. It was March 11, 1862, and the main force of the Army of the Potomac, along with their Michigan Wolverines, began their pursuit of Stonewall Jackson and his men. The Rebels beat a hasty retreat with their much smaller army eighteen miles south to Strasburg, the Wolverines biting at their heels in hot pursuit.

Meanwhile, a massive army of Federals was advancing steadily along towards a spot between the James River and the York River called the Virginia Peninsula. They were under the command of Major General George McClellan in his campaign against Richmond. McClellan ordered General Banks to leave the Valley with two of his divisions, which made

Banks extremely unhappy. Nonetheless, Banks and his men continued on to Fredericksburg, while he then directed his own underofficer, Brigadier General James Shields, to leave off his own pursuit of General Jackson at a point 25 miles south near Strasburg, and to fall back and return down the valley and maintain a secure spot, which he did in Winchester. Meanwhile, when Stonewall Jackson's scouts reported the withdrawal of Federal troops, Jackson marched his men back the same 25 miles that day and 16 miles more the next day to arrive at Kernstown, just south of Winchester. It was 2 p.m. on March 23, 1862, and in less than two hours a battle was to explode whether they were exhausted or not. The extremely tired troops were then deployed along a stonewall. Seeing the Federals off in the distance, Jackson mistakenly thought that the troops were the rear guard of Brigadier General Shields' men. Jackson was now ready to engage them in battle, a fiasco that would become known as the 1st Winchester.

Banks had no idea that the tables had turned. Off he went to Harper's Ferry, only an hour before the fighting started. Shields had himself been injured in pursuit of Jackson, during a small skirmish with the cavalry. The Brigadier General found himself in the hospital while his troops were left to the command of another veteran of the Mexican War, Colonel Nathan Kimball. He had the cannons prepared, and the fusillade began. Then the infantry fought, and the fight went back and forth for over two hours. A stalemate had been reached. All around Thomas Henry the regimental flags were falling fast, dropping to the ground as the color bearers were hit one after another. The color bearers were normally the first and favorite target, as capturing an enemy flag was the greatest of honors. The untried troops were also falling fast on both sides, every man fighting to the end. Thomas Henry Sheppard and the American flag he carried made it through this battle without a mark. That was not to be the case in the upcoming battles of the war.

Nightfall finally came to save the embattled, exhausted troops. The Confederates, already tired beyond belief, began their retreat, knowing that they had struck a blow against the Union. The Union troops, on the other hand, were ordered to push the Confederate army back. They also happened to be seriously exhausted, and their efforts were haphazard at best, as they trailed half-heartedly behind the Rebs for 20 miles or so.

It was eye-opening, to say the least, for both sides. Stonewall Jackson took this opportunity to retrain his troops under a major reorganization effort. They were drilled relentlessly, then marched south to Swift Run Gap, where they were joined by 500 additional cavalrymen and 8,500 more infantry, the men of Major General Richard Ewell's command. The reinforcements were a welcome sight.

The Feds, on the other hand, were completely miserable at "Camp Misery", two miles to the south of New Market. Their morale was fast deteriorating, their provisions were practically non-existent, and there were no tents. The rain, however, was plentiful.

The tide seemed to turn when Stonewall and his troops started moving southward up the Shenandoah Valley to Staunton. He turned into Rock Gap on the left, causing General Banks to yell out exuberantly that they were "Abandoning the Valley!" Sly as a fox, Stonewall planned for a victory at McDowell, keeping his left flank protected. A battle ensued on May 8, 1862, that was intense, violent and brutal, but unfortunately, indecisive. Stonewall went back to his main strategy--a stunning plan of forced marches, deception and bluff.

Not used to Stonewall's duplicity, or perhaps still unaware of it, Banks was so sure that the Shenandoah Valley was secure that he kept moving more men over to help General McClellan in his move against Richmond. Then when Shields left the Valley taking his 11,000 soldiers, General Banks was left with only 8,000 men to cover the north route, forcing him to fall back to Strasburg from New Market.

Apparently, this was what the sly fox Stonewall was waiting for, because on a very rainy May 20, 1862, he began moving the infantry into New Market, vacant now that Banks had evacuated. On May 22, and joined by Ewell's men, Stonewall Jackson made a sudden move to the east into the gap in the mountain range, leading them now hidden from Banks and heading safely down the Luray Valley, where they quickly subdued the Union army in the Federal garrison there on the 23rd, a complete crushing defeat in under an hour. Casualties were high for the Federals, causing the right flank of General Banks to be completely unprotected. Winchester held their food supply. When Banks had received his courier's report of bad news at his temporary camp at Strasburg, he replied, "By God, sir, I will not retreat!" However, there were so many wounded and sick that he quickly realized that they must be sent to Winchester. The entire army was in total disarray--wagons mixed in with ambulances of the sick and wounded, all in disorganized flight back down the Valley. On the route to Winchester, Stonewall Jackson and his men came in from Front Royal, attacking the soldiers in the rear columns. This was very haphazardly done, cavalry against cavalry. The Federal Army simply dropped everything and ran north, discarding wagons and equipment along the way, litter covering the roadway for over six miles. Banks and his Federals were running for their lives. The Confederate troops were starving, and so they stopped pursuit in favor of plundering the offloaded foodstuffs. The army of Banks was allowed to retreat to Winchester.

The obvious security and safety of Winchester lulled General Banks into a false sense of confidence. He began a relaxed and unhurried bath in his personal headquarters, oblivious to the muffled sounds of gunfire, becoming steadily closer in the night. Stonewall Jackson wouldn't <u>dare</u> attack at Winchester! But it appeared that he not only would, he was! Jackson's troops were now twice the size of the wounded Feds, who Banks again ordered north to the Potomac. Jackson's men were worn out, practically starving, ready to drop, yet he pressed them on and on in pursuit of the Yankees. They caught up with them once again at Winchester, just as the beautiful sunrise was peeking through over the misty rolling hills. It was 5:00 a.m. on May 25, 1862.

It was to be called the Second Winchester, that totally horrible murderous fight. It was so bad for the Union army that Stonewall Jackson rode among his men yelling, "Order forward the whole line! The battle is won!" And yet, for over three hours, and in spite of the Confederates outnumbering the Feds two to one, the Union held fast under the killing fire. Thomas Henry Sheppard held tight to his precious flag throughout, despite the fact that the flag he held was fired upon numerous times and received both shrapnel fragment tears and several bullet holes. And yet the Color Bearer held firm and retreated along with the rest of Banks' army as confusion turned to disorganization. They were beaten, bewildered, dismayed, horrified and outflanked. Banks saw his entire army disintegrate before his very eyes, running as they discarded everything they carried, including their weapons. Banks tried to restore order and failed. Everyone, including every wagon, horse and carriage was commandeered in the frantic frenzied flight north. They fled in a panic until arrival in Martinsburg, about 20 miles away, where sheer exhaustion forced them to rest briefly before once again scattering as fast as they could towards the Potomac. They reached the safety of Maryland after a race of 35 miles in only 14 hours.

Banks and the men remaining were now safe on the shores of Maryland. Three thousand men out of 8,500 were either dead or missing. Lost were 9,300 muskets, all their medical supplies, a huge storehouse of military equipment including several cannon. Banks was fast becoming known as "Old Jack's Commissary General". None other in the war had given up so much of the Union supplies so easily.

President Abraham Lincoln was stunned to find that the Shenandoah Valley, the central part of his strategic plan, was in the hands of the enemy. It soon became increasingly clear to the Union Commander-In-Chief that something had to be done and fast. Whatever they had been doing obviously wasn't working. The President knew that the Union forces must destroy the Confederates of Jackson and do it decisively. The President's strategy, though hastily drawn up, was sound. It was to be a huge pincer movement. With Banks reinforced, he and his new troops would get the middle part, essentially just moving up the middle of the Shenandoah Valley. Surely, the President thought, he couldn't mess that up. The army of Shields was assigned the Valley of Luray, placing his men in control of and coming in from the east. Fremont was the western part of the pincer, and adding his troops to the totals of the other two brought the total soldier count up to 64,000 men. According to President Lincoln's plan, Jackson would find himself effectively trapped somewhere between the two locations of Strasburg and Winchester. To Lincoln, the plan appeared faultless. However, he was sadly overestimating the essential strength and efforts of the three commanders, whose idea of Lincoln's plan was somewhat different, and shall we say, somewhat flawed. Their idea seemed to be a leisurely stroll on a nice May day. It was, in fact, the 31st of May.

They were all getting quite tired of fighting. The romance of war was long dead. On the other hand, the attitude of the Confederates under General Jackson was quite different at this time. Although they were always hungry, he and his men were doing just fine at their quarters, split as they were between Winchester where Jackson was currently, and at Harper's Ferry, the temporary quarters of his Stonewall Brigade. Jackson apparently didn't hear of the threatening plan until the very last moment. However, he got the Brigade to retreat immediately toward Strasburg, and as quickly as possible removed himself and his troops there also. It was a slow retreat, with the Federal prisoners leading it. Close behind came the infantry, no doubt now tired of all the walking. Next were the wagons carrying all their supplies--a seven mile trail as it moved slowly southward up the Shenandoah Valley.

Once again, a good plan went bad. Was it the tiredness of the soldiers or the lethargy of the general? For whatever reason, the 'best laid plans of mice and men' started out looking very good. Shields and his men were doing a great job guarding the Luray Valley from their position in Front Royal. The army of Fremont was approaching Strasburg at a fast rate. Just a few more hours and the third and final route of escape for the enemy would be blocked. President Lincoln would be proud of his plan. Unfortunately, Banks' idea of a forceful advance up the Valley was apparently much different from Lincoln's. He and his men hurried so slowly that they were virtually no help at all. Fremont took eight days to hurry up to Strasburg, a distance of only 70 miles. Likewise, Shield's army left Front Royal too late. Then they mistakenly moved down the road to Winchester. That misdirection left them another half day late.

Arriving amongst the gorgeous ridges of the beautiful Alleghenies just in time, the men from West Virginia, Fremont's men, were in place and ready to smash Stonewall Jackson's retreating wagon train of men and supplies, now completely exposed moving slowly up the Shenandoah Valley, but once again, for some unknown reason, the Union Jacks must have been tired out and failed to act. With no immediate pursuit, the retreat of General Jackson was complete and moved along slowly. Neither side seemed inclined to do anything more except send out the cavalry for minor skirmishes.

The last battle of the Shenandoahs was in the afternoon of June 6, 1862. Brigadier General Ashby was commanding Jackson's cavalry battling some 800 Cavalrymen of the Union, just outside of Harrisonburg. Several small battles went on right about there. The colors of the 1$^{st}$ Michigan Cavalry were still being proudly carried aloft by Color Sergeant Thomas Henry Sheppard, the flag itself somewhat lighter now due to several more holes and saber tears.

It is thought that it was somewhere here during the cavalry skirmishes that Thomas Henry Sheppard, while proudly and carefully holding high his flag, looked across at the line of cavalry facing his own line. They were prepared to fire when he realized that the man opposite him was aiming right at him, and in order not to be looking down the gun sights of the man who was about to shoot and kill him, Thomas turned his head abruptly to one side and down as the call came to "fire", and the bullet charge neatly skinned off his thick mustache and grazed his temple. When the mustache grew back later, it was pure white.

It seemed that war was getting them all down. Where strategic efforts could have made a considerable difference in results, fatigue and general disenchantment prevailed, and the end turned out much differently.

Fremont was still determined to destroy Jackson, and thus left out of Harrisonburg on Sunday the 8th of June with more men and better artillery, giving him the definite advantage. Several probes and counter-probes near Cross Keys left Fremont's left flank defeated and destroyed by a total surprise counterattack. He quickly ordered his men to dig in. They watched the last of the battle from behind their hastily constructed bulwarks, pinned down as they were.

By the next morning, June 9, 1862, the Confederate Army started nipping at the heels of Shields, who had men strung out over a large space. South of Harrisonburg, the Stonewall Brigade began a new attack at a place called Port Republic. Amazingly enough, Shields' troops determinedly held their position throughout the first assault. However, the second and third forays destroyed all they had gained, and the Confederate Cavalry chased them for over nine miles down the Luray Valley in retreat. General Banks was still timidly approaching Winchester. It appeared that he intended to go no further.

The Shenandoah Valley campaign was virtually done for, with the Valley left in Confederate hands, and General Lee was now ready to go on the offensive. It would become known as the Seven Day's Campaign. It was mid-June. Lee sent Cavalry leader Jeb Stuart on a swinging reconnaissance run all of the way around McClellan's Peninsula army, which was in fact bogged-down, his right flank isolated by the Chickahominy River. The river was swollen and about full to overflowing, leaving it impossible to cross. Lee's strategy was to order Jackson's Shenandoah Valley army to join his troops and tear into the exposed section of McClellan's army. The combined armies of the Confederacy snapped at, bit and chewed up the opposition and crushed the army of McClellan into bitter defeat. McClellan's peninsular campaign against Richmond was a total bust. Now the only thing left to him was to put his tail between his legs and slink back towards Washington in shame.

> *"It is called the Army of the Potomac but it is only McClellan's bodyguard...if McClellan is not using the army, I should like to borrow it for a while."*
> **--Abe Lincoln, 1862**

Back in Washington the Union forces had been consolidated. The 1st Michigan would now proudly bear their flag for General Pope, as they headed south along the railroad, the Orange and Alexander, that is. At some point this line would meet up with the Virginia Central at a place called Gordonsville. Pope, of course, wanted to cut off the railroad from the Shenandoah to Richmond, leaving the food supply-strapped Rebels devastated. His plan was shot to pieces as the stronger forces of General Jackson met General Pope's army, including the 1st Michigan. This engagement came to be known as Cedar Mountain, a little north of Gordonsville. This little fight put another set of bullet holes in the precious battle flag of the 1st Michigan. The date was August 9, 1862. Things were not looking good for the Union Army at this time.

In fact, it now appeared that it was the right time to attack and totally destroy Pope's army before they could meet up with McClellan and his men. And thus came the battle known as Thoroughfare Gap, August 26, 1862. General Lee had Jackson sweep around Pope's troops through the Gap. This Cavalry skirmish allowed Jackson's men to take control of the main Federal supply base at Manassas. The Confederate armies had been existing on, at best, meager rations. Hunger forced the men to rifle and rummage through all the Union supplies, stuffing everything they could into their mouths, pockets and packs. They pillaged and pilfered everything in sight, the cans and barrels of food and supplies. They also destroyed anything remaining before moving on to the old Bull Run Battlefield, a very strong position. In just a few days the battle known as 2nd Bull Run would be fought. It was on August 29, 1862, when General Pope and his men battled the Rebel Army with everything the Union Army could muster. They fought through until night, starting up again the following morning, August 30. Pope did not know it, but during the night reinforcements for Jackson's army had arrived, and his rout of Jackson's army turned on him. Staggering fire hit them in a fierce counterattack, causing them severe damage and sending them to retreat beaten and battered back to the defenses of Washington.

And still the battered and bedraggled battle flag at the head of Company E, 1st Michigan Cavalry fluttered unfurled through every battle, even though the Rebels had routed them again and again. The Color Sergeant and his battle-scarred flag had served General Banks all through the Shenandoah Valley Campaign and had shown themselves well also for General Pope through the ensuing battles there, including 2nd Manassas and 2nd Bull Run. Thomas Henry Sheppard was still relatively unscathed, other than losing his mustache and the grazing of his temple. The flag, however, was routinely losing more and more of its material as it was shredded by more bullet holes and saber tears. Still, not bad considering they had been battling such a respectful adversary--the famous General Stonewall Jackson.

A devastating blow was dealt to Sheppard and the 1st Michigan in the guise of the death of their commanding officer, Colonel Thornton Franklin Brodhead, who succumbed from bullet wounds he received at 2nd Manassas, Bull Run, Virginia, on August 30. He died September 2, 1862. It totally shocked and unnerved his men. In a letter to his wife from his deathbed, Colonel Brodhead made it clear that "General Pope was outwitted, and Porter was a traitor. Neither did his duty...and if they had done their duty as he had done his, and had led as he led, the dear old flag would have waved in triumph as he endeavored to rally the broken battalions." Furthermore, he told her that "he himself could have escaped, but he would not until all hope was gone." "Our cause is just and our generals--not the enemy's--have defeated us. In God's good time he will give us victory." ... "I hope that from heaven I may see the glorious old flag wave again over the undivided Union I have loved so well." (from the Colonel's last letter)

Despite the wicked blow that so devastated the Colonel's troops, fortunately the company got some needed relief when they found themselves assigned to what they thought would be a plush job, defending Washington for a few weeks. It was a time of retrospection--recollecting the months and battles past and seriously thinking of the men who had served in the 1st Michigan and would never go home again. As far as their time defending Washington, it was actually the most difficult and arduous time they had yet seen. They had to keep watch all of the time. The Regiment lost thirty men during this time. Mosby's Guerilla's attacked often and mercilessly, leaving the 1st Michigan incessantly vigilant.

In February, in the battle known as Opequan Creek, the Confederate Army started looking for a tear in the Federal lines. The 1st Michigan sent out a 56-man detachment to repel Stuart's men, who attacked, seeing such a small force. That was a mistake! Fifteen of Stuart's men lay dead when the detachment of the 1st Michigan pulled back with no loss to themselves.

Sgt. Sheppard was reassigned to recruitment back in Michigan in September. He had done quite a bit of recruiting before, in the lull between early battles, always at Colonel Brodhead's side. It would be very different now that the Colonel was deceased. Fortunately in November Sgt. Sheppard was allowed to go home to the Thumb of Michigan on a much-warranted furlough. Thomas and Louisa and the children enjoyed a well-deserved reunion. The child thus conceived would be born in due time and named Franklin Thornton Sheppard after the gallant and brave soul who was shot at 2nd Manassas, Thomas' much respected commanding officer. Soon enough his furlough ended, and Thomas again joined the 1st Michigan Cavalry Regiment and the Army of the Potomac in the defense of Washington.

The Army of the Potomac was commanded now by General Joseph Hooker. It was the spring of 1863. It had been relatively quiet in the capital city. Hooker had taken over the Potomac Army upon General Burnside's death during the tragic defeat at Fredericksburg at the end of December. He was again attempting to capture the capital of the Confederacy at Richmond. It was clear that Hooker had skillfully reorganized the army, and morale was up. He had moved to Fredericksburg with over 134,000 Federal troops. The plan was to hold Lee and his army there. Meanwhile, the main army with Hooker planned to move west and cross the Rappahannock River, where the two armies would march united to Richmond.

Both sides were playing the guessing game--trying to second guess their enemy. Lee was planning on taking the big step of invading the North. That way he hoped to stop the Union from invading Richmond. Back he went through the Shenandoah Valley to the north. He was ready and preparing his army to cross the Potomac River on June 3. His other Confederate army, Jeb Stuart's Cavalry, around 10,000 soldiers strong, was fighting against the Union Cavalry of a somewhat equal number on June 9 at Brandy Station. It was during this fight that the Union Armed Cavalry gained much respect as the two cavalry units exchanged a saber charge on horseback.

Meanwhile, General Lee was emptying Winchester of the remaining Union forces there by the middle of June, readying his forces to invade Pennsylvania. Mostly the Rebs were going to forage the fertile fields of the North for much desired grain and meat, and then sit back and spend a short time enjoying having enough food to satisfy their constant hunger.

# THE FURY OF GETTYSBURG
## Pennsylvania

The first Union troops to enter Gettysburg came on June 28th. They were the Michigan men, the 5th and the 6th Michigan, coming right along up Emmitsburg Road. There had been an early morning rain, leaving everything bright and clean in the lovely colors of summer. The sunlight reflected in the haze, leaving quite a picture show. It was wonderful to be alive. It was even better to be jogging along with no one shooting at them. Their arrival in Gettysburg was wonderful, the streets were lined with cheering people. 'Twas just the week before when the straggly, ragged bunch of Confederates had marched through town with General Ewell. The Union Army must have looked like "knights in shining armor". The people of Gettysburg wanted some reassurance from the Union Army. Church bells were ringing, flowers were thrown and garlands were put over the horse's heads by happy girls of the town. The horses found themselves in knee-deep clover, according to Major Kidd, and "it made the poor, famished animals fairly laugh." The curbs were filled with women handing out slices of delightfully fragrant breads, lavishly covered with butter from tubs of home-made apple butter. The men and the animals must have thought they had died and gone to heaven. War had never been like this. Turning right from the center square in Gettysburg, the Michigan men made camp in lovely shaded cool groves and rich meadows. The horses were once again knee-deep in clover. Not the slightest indication of the blood that would soon run and turn the trampled fields red.

They found no enemy in Gettysburg, so the Michigan men left to return to Emmitsburg, replaced by Buford's 1st Cavalry, who made enemy contact on June 30th with rebels west of town. If the men from Michigan and their happy horses had stayed only one more day, "it would have been their destiny instead of Buford's to open the big show." (F.B. Woodford)

In Emmitsburg, much important news awaited the Michiganders. Back in Washington, an extremely unhappy President Lincoln was replacing General Hooker with General George C. Meade as Commander. Lincoln was very displeased with the timid way Hooker met the last invasion. It would remain to be seen if Meade would impress the President as the new head of the Potomac Army.

But there was something that was much more interesting news to the men of Michigan. Along with Meade at the top, the Michigan Cavalry Brigade had been given new commanders, along with the 3rd Cavalry Division. The Division went to a West Pointer by the name of Kilpatrick, promoted from the colonelcy of the 2nd New York Cavalry to the rank of brigadier general. The 1st Michigan was added to the brigade at this time, and the newly formed brigade then went to a man from Michigan named Custer. Our story of the flag now merges and becomes the story also of General George Custer.

The brigade now had four regiments: heading up the 1st Michigan was a Detroit man, Colonel Charles Town; the 5th was under Colonel Russell Alger from Grand Rapids; the 6th was headed up by another man from Grand Rapids, Colonel George Gray; the 7th was run by Colonel William Mann of Detroit. A six-gun battery of horse artillery, Battery M, 2nd U. S. Artillery under Lt. A. C. M. Pennington, also accompanied them.

Meanwhile, the Confederate Army of General Lee was gathering in somewhat of a loose crescent shape 45 miles long, from York on the east, Carlisle on the north, and Chambersville on the west. Come June 28, Lee was in deep despair, because he had not heard a word from Jeb Stuart and the Cavalry. They were normally very dependable. Dispatchers were sent to everyone under his command to begin closing the arc, moving on in towards the center and coming together about in the middle at the little town of Gettysburg. Lee knew that his old West Point classmate, General Meade, was near Camp Frederick in Maryland.

By June 29th, the Michigan Brigade could be found in Emmitsburg. They soon were off, sent out to the east along with Gregg's and Kilpatrick's divisions. They had heard reports that Stuart and his entire corps along with a long captured wagon train were somewhere in the vicinity, using side roads to try to sneak northward, hoping desperately to meet up with Lee's army somewhere to the northeast of Gettysburg before the Union Army met up with them.

The Cavalry of the Union found them, and they proceeded to nip and bite at Stuart's flank. They made them fight here and there, gaining exactly what they wanted, to annoy the Confederate Army into making a large detour through another little town called Hanover, which was 14 miles east of Gettysburg. This detour forced Stuart to go all the way to Carlisle in his frantic search for Ewell, who was somewhere else altogether--with Lee's army near Gettysburg itself.  Stuart ended up not arriving in Gettysburg until July 2nd.

Kilpatrick's men were scattered, and the Michigan men were working along the Hanover Road near Gregg's division.  The date was June 30th, and the men from Michigan were tearing at Stuart's heels when they got their first sight of their new boss.

"The brigade could scarcely believe what it saw.  The men blinked with amazement.  Custer was a monument of splendor, a sight to behold.  The dusty, road-worn troopers thought perhaps there had been some mistake: it was no soldier who had been sent to them, but a character out of some comic opera.  He was dressed in a uniform of his own contriving, the likes of which had never been seen by this Union army.  His trousers and short jacket were black velvet, with loops and ropes of gold braid or 'lace', which almost covered the sleeves and splashed in a cascade down his trouser seams.  He wore a blue navy shirt turned down over the collar of his jacket, with a flowing Windsor tie or neckpiece of brilliant crimson, tied in a large careless bow, the ends loose over his chest.  All this finery failed to hide the double row of brass buttons arranged in groups of twos, the mark of a brigadier general.

"Custer's boots were knee length, of soft and highly polished black leather with golden spurs.  His hat was soft, adorned with a gold cord.  The wide brim was turned up on one side and fastened with a rosette encircling a silver star; the other side was turned down, giving him a rakish, piratical air.  He wore his golden hair shoulder length, and a blond, full mustache drooped on either side of his mouth.  A shining sword and an elaborate belt completed this portrait of cavalier grandeur." -<u>Father Abraham's Children</u>

Maybe the men of Michigan thought Custer was trying to win the prize for the gaudiest costume with Jeb Stuart.  However, when the fighting was heaviest, Custer was a 'slapdash' fighter who charged ahead of his men.  They had no doubt where they were to be or where they were to head for to rally round their flag.  It was impossible to miss Custer, that was for sure.  His men did not laugh behind his back for long, if they did at all, for Custer was a sound and respected leader.  His troops respected him.  Soon enough that respect turned into something more…a kind of reverence.

Color Sergeant Thomas Henry Sheppard had the distinct privilege of riding at the head of his regiment right behind the general, proudly holding his precious American flag. Custer was only 24 years old, two years out of West Point. He won his stars, although he was no great guns as a scholar at West Point. He was brave. He was hot-headed. He was energetic. Some say he was immature. James Kidd was to serve under him throughout the war. In Kidd's own words, "He was not...reckless...No man could have been more careful of the comfort and lives of his men. His heart was tender...he was kind to his subordinates, tolerant of their weaknesses, always ready to help and encourage them. He was brave as a lion, fought as few men fought, but it was from no love of it. Fighting was his business; he knew that by that means alone could peace be conquered. He was brave, alert, untiring, a hero in battle..." "He was cautious and wary, accustomed to reconnoiter carefully and measure the strength of an enemy as accurately as possible before attacking. More than once the Michigan brigade was saved from disaster by Custer's caution."

June 30th was about to end. The Fury of Gettysburg was upon them. Some call it the accident of Gettysburg. No one went there planning a battle. Indeed, some of them were looking for shoes and boots to replace their worn-out ones. President Lincoln and General Meade were in agreement that it didn't matter where the two armies met in the North, but that Lee's army must be destroyed. Meade planned to position his army between Washington and wherever Lee's army happened to be. Knowing that Lee had no supply line to the South, Lee and his army must fight or retreat.

The opening day of "The Fury of Gettysburg" began on July 1, 1863, at around 5:30 a.m. and "The Fury" did not end until the end of the day, July 3rd. Pvt. Robert Chase would never forget the fight at Little Round Top, in Wheat Field and Peach Orchard. "The hoarse and indistinguishable orders of commanding officers; the screaming and bursting of shells, canisters, and shrapnel as they tore through the struggling masses of humanity; the death screams of wounded animals; the groans of their human companions; wounded and dying trampled underfoot by hurrying batteries; riderless horses and the moving lines of battle. A perfect hell on earth, never perhaps to be equaled, certainly not to be surpassed nor ever to be forgotten in a man's lifetime. It has never been effaced in my memory, day and night for fifty years."

Lt. Haskell of Meade's Army reporting on July 2, 1863: "Men were dropping, dead or wounded, on all sides, by scores and by hundreds. Poor mutilated creatures, some with an arm dangling, some with a leg broken by a bullet, were limping and crawling to the rear. They made no sound of pain...a sublime heroism seemed to pervade all." Federal lines were still strong after Lee's piecemeal attacks.

Obviously, General Robert E. Lee chose to fight, and what a fight it was! The two armies fought all over, back and forth, skirmishing here and there. The Army of the Potomac consisted of almost 85,000 soldiers under the command of General Meade. Robert E. Lee's Army of Northern Virginia was about 75,000 men. This battle raged over the three days of July 1, 2, and 3rd. It ended in a climax known as the heroic Pickett's Charge, which <u>almost succeeded!</u>

According to Captain William B. Rawle, who was there that day and gave this description in an early edition of Sterrick's "The Battle of Gettysburg", Jeb Stuart and his Cavalry were "secretly positioned about three miles east of Gettysburg at the rear of Meade's army along Cemetery Ridge. A surprise attack was planned to coincide with Pickett's Charge that might well have changed the tide of battle. However, their presence was discovered just in time as their cavalry attempted to cross an open stretch of ground between two woods. With this discovery by Union Cavalry, who prepared to attack at once, Stuart had no choice but to fight on this ground." (L. Sheppard's account in *The Dearborn Historian*). Federal cannon awaited on the crest of the hill, and it raked the Confederates marching at slow march step...like practice firing...each shell burst knocked down ten men.

*"The Enemy (Stuart) quickened his pace, first to a trot, then to a gallop, and then the charge was sounded. The nearest available compact body of Union Cavalry at hand to meet the enemy was the 1st Michigan Cavalry of General George Custer's brigade. It was ordered to meet the enemy's charge by a counter-charge. Although the Confederate brigade outnumbered the Michigan regiment, their spirited attack stopped the onslaught of Stuart's troopers and effectively cut off his chance of wrecking havoc on Meade's rear!"*

In "one of the most daring exploits in the history of warfare", Pickett's Charge, Major General George E. Pickett, under Stuart's orders, led his 15,000 Confederates up Cemetery Ridge in a desperate attempt to wrest victory for the South. The Union forces there numbered 5,000 men, which was unknown to Stuart. But the Confederate ammunition was defective, the shells exploding off the mark, which was impossible to see until the dust settled. On the other hand, the Union marksmanship was definitely superior. "The Wolverine's Spencer repeating carbines helped the 5th Michigan offset the South's numerical advantage until their supply of ammunition was exhausted." (Baldwin) Stuart called on his two best brigades, Fitz Lee's and Hampton's, to take out the Feds, which he had no doubt they would do, for they were the pride of the Confederate cavalry. No assignment had ever been too tough for them. They settled into their saddles, and then the mass of gray cavalry moved at a walk forward through the empty field at Rummel's farm, ¾ of a mile wide open. Gregg's regiments were scattered, but the complete 1st Michigan were right there behind a row of trees. Out then stepped the First, along with a few from each of the other regiments, 5th, 6th, and 7th, outnumbered as they were with the attack force of at least five to one. The enemy was also in a superior position. Still the First Michigan advanced to the charge of a vastly superior force with as much order and precision as if going upon parade. (Report of George Custer) General Custer rode to the front of the First and its support. As if some one gave a signal, both the Feds and the Rebs began to move toward each other faster and faster. It was a cavalry charge of the utmost in classic beauty and style. The Men in Blue and the Men in Gray from all over the area not on horseback actually stopped fighting to watch, for it was such a magnificent sight to see. Both cavalries continued forward, the distance lessening. One Union officer predicted, "We will be swallowed up". And then Brigadier General George Armstrong Custer, in basically his first major cavalry attack with the Michigan men, appearing as almost a thing of beauty, striking as he was, magnificent in his velvet pants and in his gold braid, rose in his stirrups, pulled out his sword and shouted, "Come on you Wolverines!"

According to one soldier, "with a fearful yell the 1st Michigan Cavalry rushed on, Custer riding four lengths ahead". The company bugles blasted the charge. Hampton's cavalry replied. Then both sides, at full gallop, flags flying, swept toward the other side non-stop, while the 5th struck at the right flank and the 6th and 7th charged the left. The men's sabers were out.

"The 1ˢᵗ Michigan Cavalry went through the staggering Confederacy 'like a knife through butter', scattering the gray horsemen like ten-pins." The very earth shook from the mighty drumming of thousands of horses' hooves pounding Rummel's farm fields. Eyewitnesses that day report that "every man was yelling like a demon". And then a sound so horrible sounded, so loud it drowned out the guns and cannons down in Gettysburg itself, where Pickett was sending his brigades up to Cemetery Ridge. The totally horrifying sound was rolling, increasing in volume, deafening--as the Blue and Gray crashed into each other going at full gallop. "It made so much noise that it sounded like the crashing of timber", claimed one witness. It actually appeared as if a mighty explosion had rocked the entire farm, as horses slammed into each other and went flying, while others upended. One can only imagine what happened to the men, trampled into the very ground. The horses screamed in agony, as did the men. (from Biel's The Civil War regarding this charge): "Men fire into each other's faces not five feet apart. Bayonet thrusts, saber strokes, pistol shots, men going down on their hands and knees, spinning round, like tops, throwing up their arms, gulping blood, falling, legless, armless, headless. There are ghastly heaps of dead men."

Those who lived through that charge got up in the spreading dust cloud and began wildly slashing out with their sabers. The ensuing battle moved up and down the length of Rummel's field, one side pushing forth stabbing and chopping, then seemingly being pushed back by the other side. This process repeated over and over. Small skirmishes started up all over on both sides, like little fires that could not be put out. One side captured prisoners, only minutes later they were again set free, while some surrendered in one area, then the other side freed them once again. Cries rang out for mercy, while shrill sounds of rage were also heard.

It was a fight man to man, with no shots fired except the occasional blast of guns and canisters. It was mainly a sword fight to the finish. There were no gentlemen at the farm known as Rummel's on July 3ʳᵈ. These fighters were hacking at each other to the death.

Meanwhile, McIntosh's brigade was attacking the Confederate army, ripping at them along the flanks. Whenever an officer appeared, they gathered up a bunch of men, perhaps only a dozen or so, who kept charging the Gray mass, terribly annoying them, biting here and there, stabbing, slashing at them. Col. Hampton, CSA, got in the way of a saber in these skirmishes. The resulting saber slash aside his head sidelined him from any further fighting that day.

Their new Brigadier General Custer, the "Boy General", was unrelenting, keeping his men attacking the Rebel army even as the Confederate brigades were falling apart. And then, all of them just plain worn out, both sides began to withdraw. According to Pennsylvanian Colonel Brooke-Rawle who saw the whole thing from a distance away, "The successful result of this magnificent cavalry charge was attributed by the victors (Union) to the steadiness and efficiency with which they used the saber en masse against greatly superior numbers of the enemy, many of whom had exchanged that weapon for the revolver."

A shocked General Lee, with his hat in his hand, rode out to meet the tattered remaining men, and said "It's all my fault! It's all my fault!" "It was all my fault--now help me to save that which remains."

And yes, General Stuart also knew it was over, they were defeated. His men had inadvertently entered a death trap. As he looked over the fields for the Union position, he saw some of Gregg's brigade coming closer, having missed the fight. His men were tired, the horses were tired, and the Federal cavalry was demoralizing them. Both sides claimed victory. The Rebel army claimed victory because they had not lost ground, while the Union Army had stopped Jeb Stuart.

Everyone agreed that "the laurel wreath went to Custer and his valiant Wolverines". Stuart was stopped from attacking the Federals in conjunction with Lee's attack, and he did not turn Meade's flank. Up at the crest of the ridge above Rummel's farm, Stuart must have known that Lee had failed, as the noise of war ended. It was twilight when he led the beaten men in his brigades back to the York Pike. Custer gathered his men and rode to Kilpatrick. The troopers of the Michigan Cavalry Brigade could sit tall in their saddles.

In his official report on the battle, Custer stated, "To Colonel Town, commanding the 1st Michigan Cavalry, and to the officers and men of his regiment for the gallant manner in which they drove the enemy from the field, great praise is due." (Baldwin) "I cannot find language to express my high appreciation of the gallantry and daring displayed by the officers and men of the First Michigan Cavalry. They advanced to the charge of a vastly superior force with as much order and precision as if going on parade, and I challenge the annals of warfare to produce a more brilliant or successful charge of cavalry than the one just recounted." (M. Maben)

Also according to Maben on Cavalry Tactics: "Interestingly, the 1st Michigan violated one guideline for a cavalry charge in the manual: in part 2, page 64, the manual states, 'In charging infantry, the troopers shout; against cavalry, silence is recommended.' Apparently Custer chose to overlook this error."

Sgt. Thomas Henry Sheppard, Color Guard for the 1st Michigan Cavalry, had proudly led the counter-charge with his bullet ridden flag held high, following his new commander, General Custer. This gallant effort stopped the secret charge of Stuart's men, as the 1st Michigan Cavalry followed their Union flag and its Bearer into this ferocious battle, literally saving the day and the battle for the Union Army. Their battle flag, however, filled as it was now with 72 bullet and saber holes, had seen its final battle, as had the proud man carrying it. It was here that the flamboyant Brigadier General and the gallant Color Bearer were to part company after an acquaintance of only four days. Our story will follow the flag. (You must look to the annals of history to follow General Custer). Color Sergeant Thomas Sheppard had been gravely wounded with a bayonet injury to his right foot and a saber slice cut right to the bone in his upper right arm, as he was knocked from his horse. Later he only remembered passing out from the intense pain, and when he came to, his first thought was for the company's American flag. He reached out and tore it from the staff, then stuffed it inside his shirt before passing out again from the pain. When he awoke he found himself in enemy hands. The fallen of the 1st Michigan Cavalry were gathered up along with other prisoners and taken to the prisoner collection point. Thomas was given no medical care and was instead marched most of the way south to Richmond.

This battle gave new meaning to the term 'killing fields'. Their colors were blue and gray, but their blood ran the same bright red. General Meade lost 23,000 soldiers, killed, wounded or prisoners. Lee and the Confederacy lost more than 20,000 men. One can only imagine in utter disgust the image of the blood-soaked fields.

General Lee looked sadly out over the miles of the dead as he ordered his own wounded onto the wagons. The prisoners of war were mostly left to march along as best they could.  Aside from that, Lee's only thought was of escape.  With the remaining cavalrymen riding guard, the escaping wagon train was a totally unbelievable 17 miles in length, as it slowly lumbered on its way to Chambersburg.  One of its captive prisoners was the Color Guard of the 1st Michigan Cavalry.  No one tended to his wounds.  No water was given.  At first Thomas held out hope that a rescue effort might be made by his comrades in the Michigan Cavalry.  He did not realize the extent of the dead and wounded men destroyed at the battle at Gettysburg.  His participation in that event had him positioned about three miles out of town and alongside a ridge, unable, really to see much other than the spot he was in.  He would only hear bits and pieces of the overall story later in prison.  As the wagon train reached their destination of Chambersburg and kept right on going, through the gap known as South Mountain, and on to the south, the prisoners could only assume from small snatches of overheard conversation amongst the Rebs that they were headed for the Potomac and Virginia.

Lee's retreat of the uninjured infantry and cavalry was marching down Hagerstown Road, taking a direct route.  When General Meade realized that the Rebel Army was retreating, he sent off a speedy pursuit.  Alas, they took a different route and arrived at Williamsport too late.  Lee had gotten his men across the Potomac as once again the Federals let the Confederate army slip through their grasp, much to the consternation of President Lincoln.

> *"We had them within our grasp.  We had only to stretch forth our hands and they were ours.  And nothing I could say or do could make the Army move."*
> Abraham Lincoln, on the failure to pursue Lee's
> army after the Battle of Gettysburg, 1863

# THE CONFEDERATE PRISONS
As "visited" by Thomas Henry Sheppard

## LIBBY PRISON
### RICHMOND, VIRGINIA

The Virginia Central Railroad transported some of the wounded prisoners at least part of the way to the capital of the Confederacy at Richmond, packed as they were like sardines. The Color Sergeant unfortunately was forced to walk most of the way to Richmond, with no medical help for his wounded foot or arm. He was incarcerated first at the end of July at Libby Prison, which was a flea-infested and stifling old tobacco warehouse next to a canal that ran into the James River.

Libby was a terrible bad place, but it was to be Thomas' home for several months. More than 1000 Union soldiers were confined in eight large rooms. Thomas was close to death at this prison when a friend in Union Blue was likewise captured and sent to Libby where he found Thomas suffering in great pain. His wounds had been untended and were filthy, festering and badly infected. His friend tore his own shirt for bandages and cleaned the wounds as best he could.

At the tobacco warehouse, the prisoners found the food to be poor, but the water was very good. Since they were confined inside in July, the thought of being outdoors ate away at them. According to Ransom's Diary, three would sleep while one stayed awake to watch for Raiders. The first week the prisoners met the infamous "Majah Tunnah", who was sent in to search the prisoners. They were all stripped naked, their clothes carefully searched and overhauled, while the "Majah" removed absolutely everything of value he could find, returning only the clothes. Thomas' precious flag had to be carefully hidden.

It was here in Libby Prison that the men first met up with the 'N'Yarkers' or raiders who "infested every prison, and were almost as great a terror to the poor prisoners as their inhuman keepers".

Sometimes the prisoners could make the time pass by telling stories...they didn't have many stories, so the first time they heard one it was good...the second time okay...the third time the story was boring but better than nothing...by the next time it was getting very stale.

As bad as conditions were at Libby Prison, they were to find that it was better than Belle Isle. At least they were inside at Libby. Unfortunately, they were usurped by more important prisoners of war, the Union officers, who were to take over the flea-ridden old tobacco warehouse.

## BELLE ISLE PRISON
### RICHMOND, VIRGINIA
### JAMES RIVER

Belle Isle Prison was opened so that the captured Union officers could be confined together in the old warehouse called Libby Prison. Thus, Thomas Henry and the others had to move out. Belle Isle was the small island in the James River. Belle Isle Prison was just across the James River from Libby. It was a tented prison, and it was the place that Thomas Henry Sheppard would finish out the months of 1863 and into 1864. As winter came, the days were becoming endless, the flimsy tents were becoming totally uncomfortable, and probably at least half of the men did not even have tents and had to just sleep on the ground. They were lucky if they had a blanket of any kind. The food rations were next to non-existent, and the sanitary conditions were totally appalling. Newly-captured prisoners had come in on slow-moving railroad cars, packed to the gills, making their entire trip to Richmond uncomfortable and more than tedious. All prisoners were left off at the end of the "long bridge" and ordered into lines. The James River island was across from Richmond, covering about twelve acres. It was a cold, bleak piece of land which picked up all the biting winter winds as they had a clean sweep right up the water. The prisoners were turned into a pen enclosed with a ditch which was the "dead" line (if you crossed this line you were dead--they'd shoot you). And everywhere there were the gray backs (lice), crawling all over the men all the time, even while the men were freezing and more than half-starved.

One day's food ration was half a pint of rice soup and a quarter pound loaf of corn bread, made from bad meal, musty, coarse, and stinky. The rice was boiled in river water, no seasoning, no salt, and so little of it. Eight sticks of four foot wood given to every 100 men, which divided up gave each person nothing. A little coffee could be boiled out of bread crusts, if several of the men put their wood ration together. In the November cold, many men had little or no clothing. It was not unusual to find in the morning that someone you knew had frozen to death.

The sick were taken out every morning, either to town or to the hospital. They were only taken to the hospital when there was no chance of recovery. All the prisoners had heartburn and upset stomach, for which they would drink a weak tea made of lye from ashes.

ESCAPE? All talk--there was no chance of escape. The prison was well-guarded with artillery all around.

According to Ransom's Diary, (he was also at Libby and Belle Isle and Andersonville and his sharing of his story of life in the prison system of the South means we have details to share here) the Commander was Lt. Bossieux. He had two rebel sergeants who were very cruel when angered. Ransom bought a large blank book with good hoarded Yankee money. He would use it to write his diary. A prisoner could also buy extra rations--twenty cents in Yankee script was worth $2 Confederate.

Thomas' state of mind matched most of the prisoners there, downcast, thinking mostly of home and food. Thomas' thoughts were often of home back in Michigan, of his wife, Louisa, and of his little newborn and the other eight children. The feeling of his American flag pressed close to his body was, no doubt, comforting. The men would sing, tell stories, even dance some times. Some nights they got wood--those were the good nights. The nights were long, the later quiet filled with moans and sounds of utter despair. Friendships were good, for tents were shared by several men, and when a man in one group died, the vacancy was quickly filled. The gray backs, a nicer name for the vermin known as body lice, were always a problem, even in December. All over the camp the prisoners had to start at about nine in the morning, mostly stripped of their ragged clothing as they would pick off the evil bugs and kill them. Since the entire ground was crawling with them, it was an almost impossible task.

All the time they were told to be ready for a general prisoner exchange...a thousand men a day. Instead, every day more came in, 500 new prisoners at a time. Notes came in packed in the clothing issued-- notes from the ladies who had made the socks. The encouraging notes made their days. Supplies were constantly being sent from the North. Unfortunately, they mostly made the rebel officers fat!

A record of life in prison recorded meal varieties.  Food twice today: buggy bean soup, a small piece of corn bread.  All of the prisoners were hungry all the time.  A spoonful of salt one day was heaven.  No food today.  Almost all of the men stole from each other.  Some men had a little money.  A sutler set up shop on the island and sold things to the prisoners:  sour milk for $3/quart; poor brown sugar @ $8/pound; eggs $10/dozen; cheese $10; butter $11; oysters $6 per quart.

At least a hundred men were limping because their feet were frozen.  They were carrying on and crying like children.  Most of the prisoners now were barefoot.  Men were dead each morning from being chilled to death.  Clothing had supposedly been issued regularly by officers who came over from Richmond, but the Rebel soldiers seem to be wearing most of it instead of the men in prison.  Then one of the men in their tent was called to help issue clothing.  That worked a lot better, for then some of their own men got two or three things they really needed.

The prisoners kept hearing rumors of exchange of prisoners.  The men simply could not believe that their government will leave them in the Rebel prisons.  Women from Richmond often visited the prison to see the "blue coats".  Sad to say, they laughed at their pathetic condition.  They thought it so comical and ludicrous to see the men crowd the bank next to the cook house, looking at the piles of bread.  The women called them wild men and hungry dogs.

Sleeping and living conditions were incredible: nine men in a little A tent…"we had little cover, lay on the ground, putting our feet under each other's arms to keep them from freezing.  No language is adequate to convey the least conception of the awful misery and suffering endured on that island."  Many were the men who starved to death; many were the men who went insane from the exposure, the hunger, the misery.  "Men, more ghastly than death itself, were stalking around the camp, not knowing where they were wandering, with feet frozen hard."

America's Poet Walt Whitman said, after seeing some men who had just left Belle Isle, "Can those be men?"  "Those little livid brown, ash streaked, monkey-looking dwarves?  Are they not really mummified, dwindled corpses?"

The men were constantly encouraged to save themselves from all the misery and suffering simply by renouncing the old flag and joining up with the Rebels. In exchange for doing this they were promised freedom and money, but the prisoners told them they'd rot first (which many of them did).

The "tents" of ten or twelve men would set rules. Anyone who did not follow the rules was booted out of the tent. The rules were fairly simple: get rid of your lice daily; exercise; keep clean; laugh often; do not get despondent; drink no water that was not boiled. The ragged men were in deep despair, thinking as they were about their future. It was to be up to FATE to step in once more.

The people of Richmond were becoming more and more afraid of a prison break as the number of prisoners was fast increasing. The food supply all over the South was in a serious shortage that was getting worse by the day. If the Union forces were to attack, having a lot of prisoners in Richmond was a real liability. All of their able-bodied men were off to war elsewhere, leaving few to guard the prisoners. After many heated debates, they finally ruled out several locations and settled on a place called Andersonville.

## ANDERSONVILLE PRISON
### World-Renowned Hell Hole
GEORGIA

*"War does not determine who is right, only who is left."*

Thomas and his friend were among the very first prisoners to be transferred over the SouthWestern rails to the South's newest prison facility known as Andersonville. Supposedly there would be greater security and more abundant food. It was Sumter County, Georgia, near a little village called Anderson. Back at Belle Isle they were in the group that was called to gather up their personal possessions. They were then marched by the guards down to the depot to go to an undisclosed location. They had been told over and over again that they were to be paroled, so they must have thought it was their time at last. They rode the very uncomfortable rails all day long and all night long, with only an occasional stop for water

77

and hard bread. As dawn broke, the train came to a rather abrupt stop. It had arrived at Andersonville Station. The miserable prisoners were marched quickly through the woods toward what seemed to be a palisaded stockade. They were halted at a frighteningly huge log gate, guarded by Confederate soldiers. The gate swung open and the first bunch of inmates were pushed inside. Their new home in HELL was here. It was just one huge pen! Thomas was one of the first to come. He was not to leave until September of '64.

The first prisoners were aligned in ranks of 50, two ranks deep, formed by hundreds; first squad, 1st hundred; total: 600 from Richmond. The first men came on the 24th of February, and of the 600, there were now 591 left of those who left Belle Isle on Valentine's Day. The nine died of disease or were shot. The next two detachments of 300 each came on the 26th. Now there were 1200 prisoners (minus the nine now dead) on 15 acres. The new and more realistic dialog went like this: "exchanged" really meant "died", and "paroled" really meant "shot by guards".

By April there were 10,000 men in Andersonville, minus the 900 now dead. Prisoners were now divided into detachments of thousands, and sub-divided into hundreds. By the end of July, the prison held 31,678 men. With an inadequate transportation system and deteriorating economic conditions, the Confederates could not provide adequate housing or food or clothing or medical care to the Federal captives.

Camp Sumter was what they called it. A dismal hole is what it was. "The Confederate Military Prison at Andersonville, Georgia". It was just another terrible pen, much worse than Libby or Belle Isle. It consisted of a strong stockade, twenty feet high, made of strong pine logs, planted firmly in the ground. The main stockade was surrounded by a similar pine log middle stockade, 16 feet high, and then another twelve feet high. This structure was initially built to hold ten thousand prisoners. The men were wet to the skin, sitting in the pouring rain, for most had no tent or only a scrap of a tent to share, and little or no clothing. Nothing to eat was frequently the only meal for the day. Then perhaps a half pound of beef, some salt, some corn meal. It wasn't long before the corn meal became ground corn cobs. And the dropsy was worsening, making the men horrible to look at, their faces puffed all out of human shape.

Ransom's Diary: "He witnessed an ugliness which his worst

imagination had balked at contriving." "This pen is turning very rapidly into one vast latrine. No water, no rations, no shelter of any kind." The men had gangrene, dropsy, scurvy, diarrhea--and also suffered robbery and mayhem. Eighteen to twenty men were dying a day. The nights were cold and damp. The heavy dew wet everything completely, and by morning the men were all chilled and soaked. Wood was getting scarce. The men were starting to fight a lot as the prisoners were turning into forlorn looking creatures.

Sweetwater Creek divided the pen. It was about three feet wide and ten inches deep. Each side was a bog of slimy ooze one hundred fifty feet wide. If you stepped in, you would be covered with slime past your waist.

The Commander was a German named Henry Wirz. Under him, punishment was his favorite word. He had chains forged, also stocks and whipping posts. If someone did not answer him correctly--they got no supper. Wirz was a "small brained, small souled, incompetent fellow, and as cowardly and cruel as he was small in all the elements of manhood. He had the respect of no one, and had the intense hatred of every prisoner."

*ANDERSONVILLE.* Even today that name sends shivers down the backs of those who hear its name. Conditions were actually much worse there than a person can even imagine. Hope was high for a quick parole for anyone who would promise not to fight again, but there again FATE intervened when a Union General, "Beast Butler", hanged a Southern citizen for tearing down a Union Flag. Jefferson Davis, the Confederate President, got mad and cancelled all paroles until "Beast" was hanged, thus leaving Thomas languishing near death at Andersonville, "reduced to a shadow" from constant bouts with extreme diarrhea.

At times, and for whatever reason, the prisoners were lined up and strip searched. They must have been given some slight notice. Sick as he was in the beginning, apparently Thomas was coherent enough at the point right before the men were stripped naked to remove the Union flag that was wrapped around his body under his ragged clothing. He buried it in the sand, right before the prisoners were to be stripped and searched. Where he found clean sand to use, no one but he will ever know, although it was early days at Andersonville. Even though all the prisoners were Union soldiers, conditions were such there that <u>no one</u> could be trusted, even the men who shared a pathetic blanket.  Probably half of them would turn on their friends for just about anything.  Even though the troops would do anything to defend their flag, giving information on a troop flag to a prison guard just might buy special privileges for many days.  *"That he ever came out alive is a miracle."*  It is as much of a miracle that his flag survived.

Obviously, despite the horrific conditions, Thomas Henry Sheppard must have simply willed himself to live through the monotony of the days.  The term Prisoner of War sounded noble, romantic and heroic.  Realistically, **"unless relief comes very soon he will die."**  Obviously, "the romance has been knocked right out of the POW business, higher than a kite.  IT'S A FRAUD!" (diary)

Conditions at Andersonville were pathetic.  Some of the prisoners were left stark naked in all kinds of weather.  It was overcrowded beyond belief.  The prisoners had insufficient rations and polluted water to drink.  The stream that ran through the prison, Sweetwater Creek, was the same area the prisoners had to use for washing and for a toilet.  If they drank it without boiling it, their faces would swell up so much that their eyes could not be seen.  Mind you, they didn't give them anything to cook with, or any utensils to use, nothing for drinking.  There was no shelter of any kind there at all when Thomas arrived.  He was one of the first.  That was probably a good thing.  At that point the first arrivals quickly grabbed up every stick, log or branch they could find and attempted to make some shelters. They were given a little wood, and perhaps a blanket to share with at least six other prisoners.  The men would stretch the blanket out on sticks for shade in the daytime, and use it for a meager cover at night.  Huddling together must have helped some.  A lot of fighting went on among the prisoners. They were all discontented, and they must have appeared to some like a pack of hungry wolves.  But in the very beginning at least the sanitary conditions were absent.  However, as soon as the first person arrived and had to drink water or defecate, the nightmare was beginning.

According to the Confederate surgeon's report in <u>John Ransom's Diary</u>, "With their characteristic industry and ingenuity, the Federals constructed for themselves small huts and caves, and attempted to shield themselves from the rain and sun, and night damps and dew.  But few tents were distributed to the prisoners, and those were in most cases torn and rotten."

More new ragged Union men were showing up daily, on the average now of about 400. Their appearance was awful, but the appearance of the "in house" men was bad. Most had long hair, which they never combed, so it was terribly matted and "full of vermin". To say the prisoners looked sickening was an understatement...sunken eyes, blackened face, rags, and obvious signs of disease. Strangely enough, oftentimes the prisoners would still sing. That, at least, must have brought them some comfort.

The men soon figured out that there were some things, albeit little, that they could do about their rotten conditions at Andersonville Prison. Some started their own business. Washing clothes and cutting hair in exchange for food rations was one good example. Food rations kept getting smaller and smaller until it was only bug soup. A few men kept diaries. A Michigan man named John Ransom, mentioned previously, filled several notebooks which he got from trading and money. He described his own illnesses like this: he was just able to drag himself around. His teeth were loose, his mouth was sore, his gums had grown down lower than his teeth and were bloody. His legs were swollen with dropsy. The ground was completely covered with maggots. Lice by the 1,400,000 infest Andersonville Prison. There were so many, the prisoners' favorite game was ODD or EVEN. A man would put his hand down inside his ragged clothing and grab a handful of lice and pull out what he could and count them. Apparently this was an original game at this prison. There was no sign of it at the other prisons, although I am sure they didn't know what they were missing. Some of these same men claimed to have trained pet lice.

Ransom's Diary continued: There was no shelter, and nothing fit to eat. Their bodies were covered with sores, the water was poison. Everywhere they were surrounded by the killer Raiders in groups of 100, ready to cut their throats anytime. Raiders (Union soldiers also) beat to death the weak of the new prisoners. No one helped them. The Raiders killed some of their own every day. The Raiders took everything they had, as little as that might be...clothing, blankets, supplies of any kind, jewelry, anything at all. If they didn't want it, they could trade it. The prisoner's own worst enemy was his own neighbor, his own regiment buddy, another Union man. God Help Us from these "Worse Than Rebels". One of the most coveted items sought by Rebel soldiers was "buttons with hens on" (an insult to the American Eagle). The Raider problem only got worse and worse--new prisoners coming in in squads of hundreds, and soon all are dead. The Raiders were worse every day...perfect pandemonium....no one is safe....*"We should be able to die in peace."* The dead wagon filled with 30 bodies goes off, some fall off... "Oh, well, we'll pick them up later." WAS EVER BEFORE IN THIS WORLD ANYTHING SO TERRIBLE HAPPENING???

> *"Only the dead have seen the end of war."*
>
> -Plato

Prisoners came to Andersonville from all over. The Fifth West Virginia Cavalry and the Second West Virginia Infantry also supplied plenty of men for this prison. A description of prison life given by J. G. Matlick of Co. B covers the horrors of southern prison life, languishing in prison as he and his friends did. Many were the men who gave up their lives there. **"No pen is equal to the task of portraying the suffering, the depths of despair and the horror experienced in these infamous dens."**

No matter how bad the situation was, one thing was certain: <u>it could and would get worse</u>. The greatest number of men in Andersonville Prison at any one time was 33,114, or about 1700 men per square acre. Over the entire time that this prison was open, a total number of 45,613 prisoners passed through the front gates of the barricaded pen known as the Gates of Hell. Of those, 12,912 men had seen the end of war, for they were not destined to leave this hole. No cause other than bad treatment had caused the high mortality rate. Sadly, the prison could just as easily have been located on a river with good sweet clean water, able to stay clean. People in the surrounding neighborhood would gladly have supplied the prison with fresh vegetables--the lack of which caused over 8000 deaths. Sweet potatoes were grown in abundance in that area. In fact, General Winder, "the fiendish old tory" had specifically been told the spot he had chosen was a very unhealthy choice. Winder answered that that was exactly what he wanted, where the damned Yankees would die as fast as they could catch them.

Each morning the dead bodies would be collected and stacked outside the barricade. They were covered with canvas, which was also their casket. They were hauled away in wagons to be buried in a cemetery half a mile away, buried in unmarked graves. Their bodies were stripped first of blankets, clothing and anything else of value…they quickly robbed the "paroled" men.

Finally, justice. Someone actually decided to try to stop the Raiders. After six of them were hung, conditions improved slightly. However, *"Only those who are at Andersonville will ever know what Andersonville is."*

And yet, there were good things: Ransom wrote in his diary: "I am able to walk although lame. I have black pepper for soups. I am as clean as any. I have good friends to talk cheerful to." and "There are some noble fellows here. A man shows exactly what he is in Andersonville."

Andersonville was situated on two hillsides with a swampy stream of slimy, scummy water running through it. It had been a beautiful stream at one point. The entire property was originally approximately fifteen plus acres, with about three acres of it swamp. It was added to later, another ten acres. Within this fence "Federal prisoners were compelled to perform all the functions of life, cooking, washing, the calls of nature, exercise, and sleeping." (Confederate Surgeon's report). "A considerable breadth of land along the stream flowing from west to east between the hills was low and boggy, and was covered with the excrements of the men and thus rendered wholly uninhabitable, and in fact useless for every purpose except that of defecation." The entire structure of the prison was poorly designed. "The excrements were not washed away, but rather accumulated in the boggy area. The volume of water (from the stream) was not sufficient to wash away the feces, and they accumulated in such quantities as to form a mass of liquid excrement." The surgeon continued by saying that whenever it rained heavily, the liquid feces covered the low ground several inches deep, after the water went down. The sun's action on this "putrefying mass of excrements and fragments of bread and meat and bones excited most rapid fermentation and developed a most horrible stench." All along this area, the very ground appeared to be alive with working maggots, feasting "in the indescribable sickening stench which arose from the fermenting masses of human filth."

Unfortunately, because the prisoners were restricted in exercise and improper diet, and by scurvy, diarrhea, and dysentery, they were unable to evacuate their bowels within the stream or its banks, and some of the excrements were at the very doors of their tents, if they were lucky enough to have a tent. Most tents had nothing in them to keep the men off of the ground. All the men found themselves succumbing to the diseases running rampant at Andersonville. According to Ransom's Diary, "We are not what you might call hungry...actually more sick and faint and all broken down, feverish. But it is starvation and disease and exposure that is doing it. "New men are coming in, bodies are being carried out. *Is there no end but dying?"*

A very unhealthy climate, to say the least. No shelter of any kind whatsoever. It had been a lovely woods, but all of the trees had been cut, the logs used for the barricade. A few small saplings and little trees were left, but when the prisoners arrived, even those were taken and used for something. There were no shade trees in the entire enclosure.

*"Silence came every day in the quiet sleep of death."*

Most of the prisoners quickly began to disregard the filth and smell, and began to forget about personal hygiene. There was no ventilation. The prisoners raided the hospital stores whenever possible, and took off with the clothes and food meant for the hospital patients.

Twenty or so died each day. At first the "hospital" was located inside the barricades. Eventually, an area outside was cleared. About 2000 patients and hospital personnel were suppressed into this space, with practically no covering of any kind from the weather, and no beds-- the men lay right on the ground. Their waste was piled close by, overrun with millions of flies. "Flies swarmed over everything, covered the faces of the sleeping patients, and crawled down their open mouths, depositing their maggots in the gangrenous wounds of the living, and in the mouths of the dead." Huge numbers of mosquitoes filled what tents there were, leaving many patients looking like they had contracted measles. Scurvy and dropsy were affecting almost everyone, also diarrhea. The effects of scurvy were all around everywhere--pale gums, pale muddy faces, feeble acting, fetid breath, swollen features, hemorrhages, spreading ulcers covered with a dark purplish fungus growth. (Surgeon's report).

The surgeon called the prisoners, "miserable, complaining, dejected, living skeletons, crying for medical aid and food, and cursing their government for its refusal to exchange prisoners, lying in amongst the ghastly corpses, with glazed eye balls starting up into vacant space, with the flies swarming down their open and grinning mouths and over the ragged clothes, infested with lice, as they lay amongst the sick and dying formed a picture of helpless, hopeless misery which it would be impossible to portray with words or the brush." "Depression didn't help matters any. It was just a sickly dreadful place. The stench was beyond anything believable. Not one prisoner was in good health. There was no fresh air."

And to make things worse, the hospital attendants, whom the surgeon could see appeared to have been chosen from the ranks of the Federal prisoners themselves, seemed to have little interest in the welfare of their patients, and in fact, stole everything they had, neglecting the welfare of their patients shamefully. Vermin, dirt and filth literally covered the bodies of the sick. Filthy rags were used over and over in dressing wounds.

And each prisoner must be asking every day, why didn't their government come for them or arrange parole? The talk of parole went on every day. Had everyone just forgotten them?

As for what the men thought about the prison guards--the prisoners thought that they should get the warmest corner in that place they often heard mentioned...HELL.

Rations in Andersonville (from another account): they might get their rations in the morning or in the afternoon, no way to tell. Some days went by with nothing at all. Prisoners were still coming in daily at a rate of about 600 men a day. They were a ragged lot, too. New prisoners would tell of the latest battles. New prisoners died the quickest. Rations settled down to less than a pint of meal, a joke of a piece of bacon, a few peas with a lot of bugs. When they were given anything to burn, it was pine wood enough to cook--and then the smoke was a black pitch which turned all their faces black.

Escape was the only thing they could think about. Thomas and his tent mates started digging a tunnel. They were using pieces of boards, an old fire shovel, also half pieces of canteens. They took turns digging alongside a lone tree trunk, carrying out the dirt. The dirt was carefully emptied into the filthy stream. Frequently the tunnel would collapse as they worked. It went straight down and then angled over towards the stockade and under. They had no idea where they were when they were underground. It was almost impossible to determine. Finally after weeks and weeks of work, and being almost caught by other prisoners dozens of times, the tunnel was done. The men hesitantly went out two by two. The night was very dark. Amazingly enough, they all made it to the outside without being noticed or captured. The men regrouped outside, after crawling very carefully past the pickets. They were out! They moved quickly and quietly through the woods as fast as they could. They were actually free...and then the shots rang out. Everyone ran and scattered. Daylight was just starting to show. Thomas Henry still had trouble with the poorly healed foot injury. He knew he would be caught. Please, please, let me find some good food first, he prayed. Then they heard the bloodhounds in the distance. It was over. The dogs would find them, and if they were lucky, the dogs would not tear them to shreds. They were caught. Put on the chain gang. The dogs would have torn into them, but the men were smart enough not to keep running. The chain gang wasn't so bad--they were given more food than they ever had before. They could sit and rest in the shade. And they actually got a <u>real</u> piece of bacon...and spring water...and elderberries to make tea for scurvy. And they all knew they would not try again. They were weaker every day, and the dogs would always find you.

By the time Thomas was to be allowed to leave, the food supply was down to ¼ of what it originally was, and everyone was sick. Someone stole his shoes, bad as they were.

Thomas remained at Andersonville Prison from March of 1864 until September of 1864, kept alive mostly due to his will to live, to protect his beloved flag. Worn down, beaten, ravaged by lack of healthy diet, still nothing could daunt Thomas' indomitable spirit. He had something to live for, something which was to keep him alive where others had succumbed--he was responsible for the company's precious flag. Keeping it from capture was how he survived the prisons. "He said he had to live to protect his flag. No better a Color Bearer could have been made."

*"And many are the dead men too silent to be real."  -G. Lightfoot*

Taken from John Ransom's Diary, the Rebel Testimony of Surgeon Joseph Jones, given at the Wirz trial:

"Hearing of the unusual mortality among the prisoners confined at Andersonville, in the month of August 1864," ...Jones asked to go there to study the situation. Some of his findings:

John Ransom's Diary, in his words:

"In April one in every 16 died.

In May one in every 26 died.

In June one in 22 died.

In July one in every 18 died.

In August one in eleven died.

In September one in every three died.

In October one in every two died.

In November one in every three died."

"Does the reader understand that in September one-third of those in the pen died, that in October one-half of the remainder perished, and in November one-third of those who still survived, died? ...the startling magnitude...the fearful disproportionate mortality of those months was largely due to the fact that it was mostly the sick that remained behind, but even this diminishes but little the frightfulness of the showing. Did anyone ever hear of an epidemic so fatal that 1/3 of those attacked by it in one month died; one-half of the remnant the next month, and 1/3 of the feeble remainder the next month?"

Other thoughts from prison, Ransom and others: "Many men of many minds, many birds of many kinds." (a favorite copy lesson at writing school in Jackson, MI.)

*"Be not overcome with evil, but overcome evil with good."*

## SAVANNAH / MELLENS STOCKADE

Atlanta was now occupied by General Sherman's Union forces, including the Michigan men, and his cavalry threatened the security of the prisons. Thomas and other prisoners were told they were to be exchanged at last. Instead, they were sent first to Goldsboro, according to an interview Thomas gave to the Detroit Free Press, then on to Macon and the government shops in Georgia, where it seemed that an exchange of prisoners was finally imminent. Everyone's spirits were lifted by the hope of going home at last. Barring that, just getting out of the hell hole of death they called "Andersonville" would be enough, for a start.

Some of "the government shops" were apparently located in Savannah. The men had been loaded into box cars from Andersonville, given about a 6 ounce piece of cornbread, then spent many days still packed into the box cars like so many hogs, no other food or water. While the train was moving, they were jolted constantly, and suffered intensely.

Conditions at Savannah were related by J. Matlick of Fifth West Virginia Cavalry. His experiences were no doubt similar to what happened to Thomas. Once they were let out of the box cars in downtown Savannah, they found themselves on a beautiful street lined with gorgeous trees. The ones who could walk were marched off to the old brick prison. The lame just fell to the ground. Soon women of the town brought them hot coffee and warm, soft bread. A wagon and guards soon returned, and the ecstatic prisoners found all sorts of foodstuffs in the wagon, and they began stuffing themselves. Then black cooks from wealthy homes came out to fill the wagons with a lot of food--as the wagons seemed to have to stop quite a bit, as if someone was feeling sorry for the prisoners. The ladies of the city came out on Sunday en masse, hundreds of them, bringing all sorts of delicacies of the season. Unfortunately, Lt. Davis was in charge, and he was one miserable S.O.B., the most inhumane kind, and would not allow the women near. The next day, the prisoners were given a lot of A tents, and the men felt like they were in heaven. The only thing missing was the food. Lt. Davis kept the ladies out of reach and refused to feed the men. Feeding them "would have been human, and the inhuman wretch forbade it." Here the men died very fast, from even just a mosquito bite, for their blood was poisoned with gangrene already. Then one day a sympathetic

Confederate colonel and his wife came by, intent on finding out for himself what conditions these men were living under. He told the men he would be sending in supplies in four days...no one believed him...and yet he kept his promise of meat and vegetables, coffee, rice, sugar and soft bread. It was such a blessing, and they continued with good treatment in Savannah for the remainder of their time there.

Finally, they were sent to Mellens Stockade for several weeks...the handsomest prison in America. They were taken in "ambulances" --we'd call them lumber wagons in a more settled country. Mellens had tents, the ground was high and grassy. There was an outstanding stream of wonderful, glorious pure clean water. Part was actually growing trees, and while it held 6000 men, it had room for 15,000 prisoners.

Food rations were given twice every day, consisting of meal and fresh beef, good and wholesome. A ¼ pint of molasses was given to each man, and some pooled theirs to make candy. Here they had plenty of time to think. At Andersonville, they had to be alert all of the time just to stay alive.

Here they could think about living again. They even starting making lists. THINGS TO DO WHEN I GET OUT: (Ransom's list)

1)  join the Masons
2)  visit all foreign countries
3)  see Boston
4)  wear silk underclothing
5)  educate myself on how to keep out of a Rebel Prison

The men at Mellens started "spending their days building air castles that always fall with a crash and bury them in debris."

Ransom said, "I tell you there are humane people the world over who will not see even an enemy suffer if they can help it. While I have seen some of the worst people in the South, I have also seen some of the very best."

An exchange of prisoners was actually going to happen, but there were few sick up north to exchange for the sick in the south. The Rebel prisoners up north said they were sent north to be fattened up in cushy prisons. How very, very sad for the P.O.W.'s of the Union North and their families. So many men did not come home at all, victims of the Southern prisons, while the North was generally known for taking better care of the prisoners.

Parole finally occurred for Thomas Henry Sheppard and his flag on November 20, 1864. He actually was to be exchanged! On December 10th Thomas was furloughed for 90 days and ordered to report to Camp Parole, College Green Barracks, Annapolis, Maryland. Thomas joined other parolees on the hospital ship bound for Annapolis. The other survivors of the First Michigan joined Thomas there, and all of them received a complete new uniform valued at $32.60. That first sight of "Old Glory" flying in the wind over the hospital ship--well, it was a sight they could not explain. "Our feelings were such that no imagination could conceive. Eyes were flooded with tears and our hearts seemed ready to burst with the joy that filled them, and when we stepped beneath that dear old flag, for which we had dared to offer ourselves a living sacrifice, we could not cheer, but we sank down into quiet weeping, thankful for escape from our living tombs." (Matlick)

Doctors finally examined Thomas, fed him well, then sent him on his way to Detroit and an honorable discharge on March 27, 1865. He was paid a sum of $99.91. He had been a Prisoner of War for 505 very long days. He and his beloved flag would now return home, only now his flag was once again held for anyone and everyone to see. "He Kept The Colors".

*"He who is guided by love of country is guarded by God."*

-L. E. J.

Thomas Henry Sheppard joyfully returned home for his first sight of his newest son, Franklin Thornton Sheppard, now 18 months old. It was bittersweet, as Thomas could not help but think again of his brave Commander, Colonel Brodhead, who had given his life at Second Manassas. After his joyful reunion with his youngest son, Thomas quickly realized that his son, Fred, was missing. Fred had gone off to war to look for his father. Thomas was out of his mind and furious. The battlefield was the last place on earth that Thomas Henry wanted his young son to be. But it was too late. Fred had enlisted into his father's own regiment, the 1st Michigan Cavalry, to go off to war to find his missing father, since the family had had no word from Thomas since his capture at Gettysburg. Freddie was only fifteen, but big for his age. He told his mother that he would run away if she would not sign for him to enlist. So, in late fall of

1863, Fred went off to war. He was 5'6", a blue-eyed blond. For enlisting, Fred received a bounty of $62. with two additional bounty payments to come later, and a month's advance pay of $13. Fred swore to bear true faith and allegiance to the United States of America, signing for a three-year enlistment. He was with Grant's men from the Rapidan to the James River, and in "the leaden hurricane of the Bloody Angle and Hell's Half Acre". He saw Private John A. Huff kill the Confederate Hero, General J.E.B. Stuart at Yellow Tavern skirmish.

Debilitated as Thomas was at that point, after 505 months of devastating prison life, his body just a shadow of his former self, he nonetheless immediately stormed back to the recruitment office to re-enlist. Due to the terms and conditions of his parole, Thomas was unable to do so. Undaunted, Thomas apparently went to another recruitment office and attempted to enlist once again, this time under another name. They must have somehow known, for he was not able to go with the 1st Michigan, but instead was sent to Washington to work in an office for the duration of the war. Family records show he enlisted in Co. A, 8th Regiment, Hancock's Veteran Corps as a recruiting officer on April 6, 1865, for a one year term. The war, however, was quickly drawing to a close as General Lee surrendered to General Grant on April 9 at Appomattox, Virginia. (Thomas' son Fred was there, riding with General Custer's unit.) Shortly thereafter, in Washington, our beloved President Abraham Lincoln was assassinated on April 14.

The end of the Civil War came officially when General Lee's Confederate army surrendered. Thomas' one-year enlistment ended on April 5, 1866, and he was discharged once again at Washington, D. C. and went home. Son Fred, alas, had returned to Washington, D. C. for the Grand Review down Pennsylvania Avenue, where Senator Chandler of Detroit congratulated the boys on a fight well fought and on the Northern victory, and sent them home for a well-needed rest. The train headed west but unfortunately had no intention of stopping anywhere near Michigan. The boys in blue found themselves at Ft. Leavenworth, Kansas, to fight the Sioux and Dakota Indians. Feeling betrayed, many of the First Michigan Cavalry volunteers simply left without discharge and went home. They had signed up for only three years, and it was up to the Army to fix things. Twenty years later, Fred was still fighting his desertion claim. In 1884

Congress passed legislation, and Fred's attorney was successful at last in clearing Fred's name of desertion status, although he was never to receive his bounty or pay. I guess you could say that Fred would be very glad that he had split company with their flamboyant and much loved General George Armstrong Custer who was to lose his life along with all of his remaining men at the Battle of Little Big Horn.

Back in Michigan, Thomas had moved his family once again, and this time settled a bit farther north in a tiny new town in the very heart of the Thumb, in the county of Sanilac, created by Michigan Legislature in 1848. Thomas came to the new little town of Marlette to join other families he knew and was related to, among them the McGills, through whom he had received his beloved flag. He bought a farm and settled the family in there. Then in 1868 he bought a lot right on Main Street in Marlette just south of where the stoplight would one day be and promptly built and became proprietor of the finest hotel in the area. The old Northern Hotel was to become a landmark to visitors and citizens alike--a place to be proud of. The Northern was located on the northwest corner of Main Street and Morris Street, and was an important part of Michigan's past. Historically, it was the second frame building built in the village. It survived Michigan's Great Fires, both in 1871 and 1881. Thomas sold out in 1872. Thomas was a Republican, a proud member of the Grand Army of the Republic, and forever a Man in Blue.

Northern Hotel

Thomas's first wife, Louisa, was driving the family carriage on November 29, 1872, when the horse bolted, and she was killed. Thomas soon remarried. She was Anna Williams, who was much younger than Thomas (in fact, she was his own daughter-in-law's sister). They were married in a double wedding with Thomas' son. Soon enough they then added to the nine children (not counting little Alice who had died) he had with four more: Robert, Effie, Nellie and Burt. Tragedy struck Thomas once again when Anna died of tuberculosis in 1882, aged only 36. Thomas quickly remarried again, as a sixty-year old with 13 children obviously needed a wife. Rachel was fifty-eight, and lived for eleven years of marriage. She died in 1899. Thomas' fourth wife was Gracia Hager Abbey.

Thomas lived 78 years. He was a "jolly" man and a "grand old man", according to neighbors.

His association with the government was a bit troubled, as he attempted to get both of his pensions for serving in the Civil War, first as Thomas Henry, and also under the name of William. He received a pension in 1884 of $4 a month. This increased three more times until 1891 when he got the impressive sum of $24. per month.

He was a proud member of the Grand Army of the Republic, Rogers Post--a group made up of retired Union Army men. He was the principal speaker at every Decoration Day program for as long as he lived. He always got a place of honor at all the G. A. R. events.

The end for Thomas came when he had a stroke while attending a neighbor's funeral at the Methodist Episcopal Church in Marlette in 1901. He was in and out of consciousness, partially paralyzed on one side. This went on for about two weeks. His old war wounds greatly pained him, and Gracia tried to comfort him with oil of mustard packs. He died on March 5, 1901. Thomas was laid to rest in the Imlay City, Michigan, Cemetery, aged 78 years, eleven months, one day.

# THE GENERAL, THE OLD MAN, AND THE FLAG

*September 13, 1884*

The whistle-stop campaign of America's much loved General John Alexander Logan for Vice-President of the United States of America took him across the fair state of Michigan by Special run of the Port Huron and Northwestern Railroad in September of 1884, stopping at every little railroad station along the way to give a brief campaign speech from the back of the train. According to the official 1884 Rail Report, the road-bed was in first class condition, and it was believed to be the finest narrow-gauge railroad in the entire United States. (The Railroad had come to Marlette, Michigan, in the very heart of the Thumb, in 1881. The little town had to raise $15,000. towards the costs to entice the railroad to come.) Although the average speed of the train that year was 30 mph, this train made an all-out effort that particular day for General Logan, making six miles in seven minutes, reaching their record speed for 1884 of 59 mph! They must have known that General Logan was running for the Vice-Presidency!

A large crowd of people had gathered to wait in anticipation at each little stop along the way, for everyone wanted to see "Black Jack" Logan, the great soldier and statesman. The train pulled into the little village of Marlette, in Sanilac County, on September 13, 1884, where a large group had indeed gathered at the railroad station. General Logan stepped out of the caboose, and everyone's hero spoke to the crowd from the rear platform of the train.

The General gave his brief and rousing campaign speech, ending as he always did with an anecdote about an unknown soldier from the Civil War. "Black Jack" Logan, himself known as the "great volunteer", told

94

his favorite tale of this nameless volunteer who marched off to war with "flashing eye and sturdy stride", proudly carrying an American flag made for him by the women of his little town. While he was talking, the General's eyes looked out over the crowd and came to rest upon a gray-haired old man standing at the far edge of the crowd, a man whose form was bent and who held in his trembling hands a worn and tattered old flag. Pausing for a moment, Logan began anew. Glancing again at the old soldier, the General could somehow picture the scene on that day when the man was young and strode forth carrying that flag at the head of his regiment. Then the General ended his speech with a flowing tribute to the volunteer soldiers of the Rebellion. When the applause had died down, he went back into his railroad car and sat down by the window. No sooner was he seated than there came a tap on the glass. It was the old man with the flag.

"General," faltered the old man through the raised window, "General, the women of this town made this old flag, and I had it with me all through the war. When I was captured, I wound it around my body under my clothes, and kept it all through my imprisonment at Andersonville Prison. I've got a little farm here worth $3000.00, and I've got this old flag, but if I couldn't keep but one the farm might go."

The tears came to General Logan's eyes as he answered tenderly: "Tell the boys Jack Logan says that when you come to die they must wind that flag around your body and bury it with you--'twill be the countersign to admit you through the gates of heaven."

Then the train moved on, and the last thing we saw was the old man standing there with his flag.

> *--William Bates, aide to General John (Black Jack) Logan regarding their trip across Michigan in Logan's whistle-stop Campaign for the Vice-Presidency of the United States (reported in the Marlette Leader, Detroit Journal)*

Thomas Henry Sheppard's old flag was not buried with him, as General Logan had suggested, although I am certain the old man made it through Heaven's Gates just fine.

Instead, his grandson donated it to the Dearborn Historical Society in Dearborn, Michigan, where it is their most prized possession. The old flag has been returned to the Commandant's Quarters of the Detroit Arsenal USA (1833-1875) at 21950 Michigan Avenue in Dearborn, Michigan, from which Thomas Henry Sheppard and the First Michigan Cavalry were armed and departed from to go off to war. It is now the Sons of Union Veterans of the Civil War.

## General Logan
### Obituary

General Logan was a member of the U. S. Grant Post #28, Grand Army of the Republic, Department of Illinois. Known affectionately as "Black Jack", he was the first Grand Commander and one of the founders of the G.A.R.

When called into service by the Angel of Death, Logan's obituary declared of Logan: in war he was in full measure the epitome of a true American soldier, always showing boundless courage in the face of danger. "Black Jack" was patriotic to the highest extreme and was universally well-loved and respected by those under his command. He was that rare human being who also treated his enemies with the utmost kindness, and he was generous to the fallen foe.

Those who knew him were likewise just as proud of his record in peace time as they were of his war record. To all eyes, it seemed as though he was loved by everyone. Throughout his public service career, even when closely watched by his opponents, Jack Logan was never found guilty of an unworthy or dishonorable act or deed. "He lived before the world, as he died, at his post of duty, an honest man." (1889 *Marlette Leader*)

General Logan showed his abilities in the hallowed hall of Congress by his wise and needed legislation on the floor of the Senate, by the debates he participated in, and by the many speeches he gave. All in all, Logan was considered one of the greatest statesmen of that era.

When the Death Angel came trumpeting to summon the great volunteer, the Grand Army of the Republic muffled its drums, pulled out its mourning clothes, and draped the flag in deepest black to show in a small way the deep regard they held for its best loved and most distinguished fallen comrade. Never before was the U. S. Grant Post such a lodge of sorrow. Never before was the post so deeply hushed. With hearts beating heavily in sorrow, tears flowed from the eyes of every bowed head, for General Logan was dead.

"Then I heard the voice of the Lord saying,
'Whom shall I send?
And who will go for us?'
And I said, 'Here I am, Lord, send me.'"

*--Isaiah 6:8*

-Dearborn Historian

# *BIBLIOGRAPHY:*

The Rest of the Story by Paul Harvey

U. S. Civil War: Battle Flag of Co. E, 1st Michigan Cavalry 1861-1865

The Commanders of the Civil War by William C. Davis

Great Battles of the Civil War by Graham and Skoch

The Widow of the South by Robert Hicks

Libby Prison, Richmond, Virginia, *Official Publication #12, Richmond Civil War Centennial Committee*

*"Prisons, Paroles & POWs" & "2004 Civil War Richmond"*

*1884 Portraits and Biographical Sketches of Sanilac County, Chapman Brothers*

IMAGES-Millennium Edition by L. E. Johnson

Best Photos of the Civil War by Milhollen and Johnson

The Civil War Sourcebook by Chuck Lawless

"A Soldier and His Flag" by Lawrence C. Sheppard

Father Abraham's Children-Michigan Episodes in the Civil War by Frank B. Woodford

Bruce Catton & John Ransom's Diary

J. H. Kidd; One of Custer's Wolverines

Saving Private Ryan by Max Collins

Andersonville by MacKinlay Cantor

The Jones Family of Huntsville Road, Birmingham, Alabama
by Leah Rahls Atkins w/ Flora Jones Beavers

The CIVIL WAR Strange and Fascinating Facts by Burke Davis

*Newspapers:*
*The Marlette Leader, The Detroit Journal, The Detroit Free Press*
Civil War Times Magazine

What They Didn't Teach You About the Civil War by Mike Wright

The Civil War by Timothy Levi Biel

The Civil War by Douglas Welsh

Commander in Chief Abraham Lincoln and the Civil War. by Albert Marrin

"Major General Alfred Pleasonton's Official Report for the Battle of Gettysburg"

"Michael Maben on Cavalry Tactics"

"General George A. Custer's 'Lost' Report of the Battle on the East Cavalry Field, Gettysburg, July 3, 1863"

"1st Regiment Michigan Cavalry"

"First Michigan Cavalry"

"Baldwin Genealogy Antrim Michigan"; Civil War Years 1861-1865

USA Flag Site

"Report of Brigadier General George A. Custer, U.S. Army, commanding 2nd Brigade & 3rd Division, Battle of Gettysburg"

One of Custer's Wolverines: the Civil War letters of Brevet Brigadier General James H. Kidd, 6th Michigan Cavalry

"Historical Times Encyclopedia of the Civil War"; Faust

# About the Author

The author was born in Detroit, Michigan, in October of 1949, the third of four children of Harold and Marjorie Johnson. Harold was from Albion, New York, where his great-grandfather had come in on the opening of the Erie Canal and settled at a place called The Bridges, New York. Harold came to Michigan to work in the automobile plants during the Depression, where he met and married Marjorie Dawson, who was in the city attending Beauty School. In 1957 they returned to her hometown in Marlette in the Thumb of Michigan and bought the family farm started by Grandfather William Dawson in 1882.

Lois graduated from Marlette High School in 1967, Salutatorian and Class Treasurer. She pursued her college education at Oakland University in Rochester, Michigan, receiving a Bachelor of Arts in Elementary Education in 1971. Although she was offered the newly-formed position of Director of Alumni at OU, it was only a half-time position then, and she instead went to work for Warren Consolidated Schools as a Math/Science teacher at Grissom Junior High on 14 Mile and Ryan, beginning her first real job walking the picket line, on strike. Pink-slipped at the end of her first year teaching, Lois returned to the Thumb and spend the next 27 years teaching Math, then Social Studies and Reading, to 6th graders, taking Early Retirement in 1998. She earned a Master's Degree from Central Michigan University, and 18 hours towards her Specialist's.

In the early 1970's she purchased 50 acres of the family Centennial Farm, turning it into a Michigan Non-Profit Wildlife Sanctuary, where she now raises beautiful free-ranging peacocks on one of the most lovely spots on earth.

In 1985, Lois happened to visit a stunning old Victorian House in town, where she was amazed to learn that it had been built by her mother's Great-Uncle, Thomas Usher Dawson, Marlette's leading businessman in the 1890's. That started her on a quest for family information that ultimately led to the town's newspaper office, *The Marlette Leader*, where she found the old copies of the newspapers. It was that visit that eventually sparked enough interest that she convinced the newspaper editor, John Frazier, to help her start *The Marlette Historical Society and Museum*. They then microfilmed the old newspapers, and had three Marlette buildings named to the State Historic Sites Registry: the Victorian House of Thomas Usher and Jennie Dawson; the Marlette First United Methodist Church, and the 1890 Marlette Depot. They wrote grants for a museum, bought the old depot and did everything necessary for its restoration, thanks to two additional grants from the State of Michigan and M-DOT. 1987 was the 150th of the State of Michigan, the 125th of the City of Marlette, and the 100th Year of the High School, which they commemorated with a 432-page book, in conjunction with the High School Yearbook, IMAGES. Lois then followed up on that book with an 820-page Millennium Edition.

She adopted 12-year old twins in 1989. She was named to Who's Who Among America's Teachers in 2000 and again in 2005, an honor given to less than 3% of America's Elementary Teachers.

She wrote of her father's friendship with the World's Greatest Santa Claus, Charlie Howard, in the book, My Dad Knew Santa Claus. Charles Howard, of Albion, New York, who unbelievably held 5 million children on his lap, was the famous Macy's Santa who started the World's Only School for Santas and the wonderland for children, Christmas Park, the unequaled Santa Claus Headquarters of the World. Howard died in 1966, when he was entered into the United States Congressional Record as the Dean of Santa Claus. It is an adult story for the child in each of us.